Suffering
SALVATION

Why Do Christians Experience Pain?

TONEY A COX

WESTBOW
PRESS®
A DIVISION OF THOMAS NELSON
& ZONDERVAN

Copyright © 2023 Toney A Cox.

All rights reserved. No part of this book may be used or reproduced by any means, graphic, electronic, or mechanical, including photocopying, recording, taping or by any information storage retrieval system without the written permission of the author except in the case of brief quotations embodied in critical articles and reviews.

This book is a work of non-fiction. Unless otherwise noted, the author and the publisher make no explicit guarantees as to the accuracy of the information contained in this book and in some cases, names of people and places have been altered to protect their privacy.

WestBow Press books may be ordered through booksellers or by contacting:

WestBow Press
A Division of Thomas Nelson & Zondervan
1663 Liberty Drive
Bloomington, IN 47403
www.westbowpress.com
844-714-3454

Because of the dynamic nature of the Internet, any web addresses or links contained in this book may have changed since publication and may no longer be valid. The views expressed in this work are solely those of the author and do not necessarily reflect the views of the publisher, and the publisher hereby disclaims any responsibility for them.

Any people depicted in stock imagery provided by Getty Images are models, and such images are being used for illustrative purposes only.
Certain stock imagery © Getty Images.

All Scripture quotations, unless otherwise indicated, are taken from the Holy Bible, New International Version®, NIV®. Copyright ©1973, 1978, 1984, 2011 by Biblica, Inc.® Used by permission of Zondervan. All rights reserved worldwide. www.zondervan.com The "NIV" and "New International Version" are trademarks registered in the United States Patent and Trademark Office by Biblica, Inc.®

Scripture quotations marked (ESV) are from the ESV® Bible (The Holy Bible, English Standard Version®), copyright © 2001 by Crossway, a publishing ministry of Good News Publishers. Used by permission. All rights reserved. The ESV text may not be quoted in any publication made available to the public by a Creative Commons license. The ESV may not be translated into any other language.

Scripture marked (NKJV) taken from the New King James Version®. Copyright © 1982 by Thomas Nelson. Used by permission. All rights reserved.

ISBN: 978-1-6642-8066-3 (sc)
ISBN: 978-1-6642-8067-0 (hc)
ISBN: 978-1-6642-8065-6 (e)

Library of Congress Control Number: 2022918955

Print information available on the last page.

WestBow Press rev. date: 02/02/2023

DEDICATION

This book is dedicated to our firstborn son. Taylor Anthony Cox was born/passed away on December 15th, 2010. One day, while in heaven's glory, I believe we will talk, laugh, and enjoy one another in a father-son relationship. This book was birthed in the anguish of his loss. Therefore, may this work bring glory to the God who healed my hurting heart.

This book is further dedicated to my mom, Cora Lee Cox (1956-2021). My mom is my hero who decided to endure the battle of blindness without fear or compromise. Her life was one of dedication to her family. A woman of sacrifice, she lived her life to support others. Her untimely suffering and death were unfortunate. However, she lives in my heart, forever motivating me to excellence.

This book is further dedicated to my grandmother, Janet Sue Cline (1937-2022). My grandmother was my second mother in multiple forms. Helping to mold my life, she left an unforgettable void when she departed this Earth. A woman with a tenacious fighting spirit, she modeled before me the attitude of a fighter in the face of challenge.

CONTENTS

Dedication v

Preface ix

Acknowledgments xi

Chapter 1 It Depends 1

Chapter 2 Free Will 13

Chapter 3 The Big Picture 27

Chapter 4 The Faith Factor 41

Chapter 5 The Trials of Life 57

Chapter 6 Spiritual Warfare 70

Chapter 7 A Talk with Dad 89

Chapter 8 The Examination Room 105

Chapter 9 Final Thoughts 120

References 129

PREFACE

The scope of this book presents a singular focus on why God permits believers to suffer. As a reader of the book, note that the work's thesis is directly focused upon the experience of the believer. This book, in contrast, does not delve in a generalized fashion concerning why God permits the existence of evil. Furthermore, this book does not stray into the aspect of why God allows suffering, in a vague form, within the fallen human race. The topic of the existence of evil, in general terms, is a discussion for a different work. Instead, this book communicates a narrow focus on the theological exploration of why God permits believers to experience periods of suffering.

In the same vein, this book is written from the soteriological aspect that a believer is defined as someone who has received Jesus Christ as savior (John 3:3; John 3:16; Romans 10:9-10; Ephesians 2:8-9; Romans 6:23). Accordingly, the book presents a repetitious reference to believers experiencing suffering salvation. Thus, this is to be interpreted as people who have been born again and have experienced moments in life that are unfortunate.

The term believer is synonymous with the term Christian. Furthermore, equivalent phrases for a believer, they (he, she) that believe (for *hoi pepisteukotes; hoi, pisteuontes;* (adj.), *Pistos*, etc.)

frequently occur as a regular description of those who professed their faith in Christ and attached themselves to the Christian church (Rees, n.d., para. 1). Therefore, the word believer is employed within this book for the specific reference to those who profess and follow Jesus Christ as savior.

A cry that has been redundant throughout the history of the church of Jesus Christ is common beyond race, ethnicity, generation, culture, or social status: Why does God allow Christians to suffer? The pain of loss is genuine within the homes of multiple Jesus-following worshippers. Likewise, the emotional torment is authentic within the hearts of numerous families coping with death, disease, and detriment even though they profess Christ as savior. Notwithstanding, God has permitted scores of believers worldwide to face martyrdom along with periods of excruciating pain. Yet, the theological question permeates: Why?

Therefore, the heart of this book seeks to disclose additional theological understanding to the existing literature coupled with the vision to provide emotional healing to the hurting heart of the believer who has experienced suffering salvation.

May it also be acknowledged that all scripture references within this book are quoted from the *New International Version* of the Holy Bible. Any other version of the Bible employed within this book is appropriately noted within the reference. In addition, this book is formatted in the current APA format.

ACKNOWLEDGMENTS

It is to be acknowledged that my wife, Monica L. Cox, equally shared the anguish of our loss of Taylor Anthony Cox. She has experienced the trauma of suffering salvation in multiple forms beyond the scope of this book. Furthermore, she has stood by my side through each experience of pain, sharing the burden that suffering bears. Thank you for your support in the sacrifice of this book and for the faithful patience displayed within the laborious effort to offer a theological response to suffering salvation.

It is to be further acknowledged that our son, Samuel B. Cox, is the light of our life and the offspring of God's grace. We are forever grateful for the gift of your presence. May this book inspire you to reach for the heights that are found in Christ Jesus.

It is to be further acknowledged that absent of God's love, grace, calling, anointing, visions, and dreams, I am nothing of an excellent report. God has loved and been patient with me beyond longsuffering. Meanwhile, the dream for this book was cast into my heart by the grace of God. Further, God helped me write this book, and for that, I am thankful.

Chapter 1
IT DEPENDS

Time and time again, the dilemma of suffering supplies a staggering blow to faith. Prominent atheists such as Richard Dawkins, coupled with scores of those who have endured chapters of suffering within life, cling to a notorious argument devoted in opposition to the existence of God. The philosophical reductio argument proposes the following sequence of ill-formed logic,

> "If evil exists and God exists, then either God does not have the power to eliminate all evil, or does not know when evil exists, or does not have the desire to eliminate all evil. Therefore, God does not exist" (Stanford Encyclopedia of Philosophy, 2015, para. 7-8).

Comparatively, similar points of view contend that God is either impotent or evil for the permission of pain,

> "A good God cannot coexist with evil and suffering in the world. Omnipotence, it is argued,

means that God is always able to act. It is immoral for such a Being to stand by and allow innocent beings to suffer when he could intervene - God is therefore either impotent or evil" (Brown, 2013, para. 10).

Notably, God is often disregarded due to the coiling of suffering, which is so frequently encountered throughout life. So frequently, in fact, that the persistence of pain and suffering commonly breathes life into doubts concerning God.

Narrowing the focus, mass numbers of believers worldwide, while trusting in Christ for salvation, repeatedly struggle in their faith over the infamous question of suffering. Undoubtedly, being born again does not invariably ensure a lack of suffering. Believers are not exempt from heartache. Suffering and salvation are commonly interlaced in an uncomfortable actuality. Therefore, suffering salvation, as labeled and defined within this book, creates room for authentic questions concerning the coexistence of suffering and faith.

In fact, multitudes of believers throughout the centuries have proposed the well-rehearsed rhetorical questions concerning suffering and salvation: Why do believers suffer? Why does God permit periods of pain in the lives of the faithful? For centuries, an undeniable number of believers have experienced agonies and heartaches. Why? Why does God allow believers to encounter such unrest and misery?

God is good. Yet, Christians experience the horror and violation of sexual rape. God is love. Nevertheless, believers encounter the pain of broken bones in the sudden shock of vehicle collisions. God is caring. However, believers often undergo the agonizing death of cancer. God is unlimited in aptitude and knowledge. Nonetheless, innocent children are slaughtered in schools. God is merciful. Conversely, faithful worshippers combat periods of painful loss.

The aching turmoil of murdered children, as experienced by Christian families, still occurs, even though God is an all-powerful being enclosed with the capacity to circumvent the action. Believers maintain faith even though they, in various circumstances, mourn over children who perish in overdose. People often love Jesus and simultaneously witness a loving spouse suffer a physical ailment. Overall, suffering salvation is an authentic quandary that presents theological inquiries for countless believers. Have you ever found yourself stung by the pain of suffering salvation?

A sundry of believing Christians have found themselves astounded by the common pain of enduring suffering, trials, and sorrowful circumstances within life. Making the faith battle even more difficult in the face of suffering is the minefield of theological persuasions. Faith teachers excessively stretch scripture, casting all responsibility of suffering salvation upon the exercise of little faith.

At the same time, John Calvin's teaching of classical sovereignty reaches the opposing margin suggesting that all events are in the direction of God and unrelated to an individual's faith or control (Calvin, *Institutes* 1, Chapter 16). The pervasive question looms: Which theological position is correct concerning suffering salvation?

As a young pastor in 2010, my wife and I experienced our first entanglement with the emotionally extensive pain of suffering salvation; our first pregnancy. While it was saturated with faith confessions and prayer, it exposed us to the interweaved engagement of suffering and faith. Following the roller coaster of emotions upon the surprising realization that our first baby was on the way, complications placed us at the dawn of a morning sitting in a labor and delivery room at 17 weeks pregnant and consulting with the area's leading OBGYN expert in pregnancy crisis. Our faith was passionate; however, our pain was palpable.

In summation, the OBGYN expert declared, with raw facts void of empathy and emotion, that he was 99.9 percent certain that our baby boy would be dead in less than 24 hours. The diagnosis was cervical insufficiency, and the prognosis was death. As he whipped his team out of the room with an air of confidence, the registered nurse requested the preferred funeral home to contact upon the before-long demise. Our faith remained resilient, but our distress and discomfort were reeling.

Shaken, startled, and suffocated with grief, we began to pray and trust God for a miracle. We chose life over death (Deuteronomy 30:19). We spoke the Word and professed faith (Romans 4:17). We came into agreement with other believers in prayer (Matthew 18:19). We taped anointed prayer clothes on her pregnant belly (Acts 19:11-12). We spoke words of faith (Mark 11:24). We rebuked the enemy (James 4:7). We believed in God with strong faith for divine intervention.

Furthermore, we had complete assurance that this would be a miraculous turnaround; we did not doubt in our hearts. Meanwhile, our baby boy did exceed the twenty-four-hour window predicted for death. Nine days later, my wife was still in the hospital. Our boy was growing and responding, notwithstanding the complications of the pregnancy! Nurses were whispering to us during the evening shift that the doctors were beginning to chatter about something unexplainable.

Still yet, on December 20th, 2010, his funeral was conducted on a cold, snowy day with Christmas looming in the background. I was a lead pastor with complete faith in the miraculous: Why was I experiencing suffering salvation? We confessed faith and believed in God for life: Why were we hurting while trusting Jesus? This was not our final suffering moment in life. Additional periods of pain emerged, as will be shared later in the book. However, this was our initial shattering experience of suffering salvation.

Have you ever wrestled with sickness or hardships that left you asking the question: Why do believers suffer? Why? Why would a good God who is omnipotent (all-powerful) seemingly hide in the stillness allowing Christian women to be raped, heart attacks to unfold upon the faithful, and murders to be committed within worshipping families?

Why do babies die? Why do believers' children overdose? Why do believers experience death in vehicle collisions? Even more, confounding is the bewilderment of cancers growing inside bodies that worship Jesus. Likewise, why are Christians martyred? Why do innocent children living in Christian homes experience abuse? Why? Why does God allow people who know Christ as savior to suffer?

These are genuine questions that scores of authentic believers ask regularly. As a lead pastor, multiple moments have been invested in extending counseling comfort to Godly believers as they cry out in pain, imploring why their loving God would permit this poignant pain to befall their lives. *The subject at hand cannot be denied.* If pastoring has taught me anything, it is that genuine believers who possess strong faith often wrestle with this straightforward question: Why do believers experience suffering salvation?

My struggle with the loss of our baby, coupled with multiple succeeding entanglements with suffering salvation throughout the years, propelled me to the scriptures in search of discovery to answer the infamous questions around faith and suffering. Overall, I had to ascertain why God permits suffering to unfold within the lives of believers. My heart hurt, and my faith struggled as we buried our baby. I was desperate for something more than a loving smile, a warm hug, and a sympathy card provided in routine by the church during our time of suffering.

Additionally, as a lead pastor, I knew that I had to be equipped with answers in my arsenal to facilitate believers during their times of suffering salvation. The pastoral response of prayer and counsel is beneficial to hurting believers. The pastoral response grants help, hope, and hospitality to the hurting heart. The pastoral response to suffering is praiseworthy and necessary in the initial stages and during the long-term stages of mental and emotional healing.

This approach offers the hurting believer in-person visits, cards, food, calls, texts, and other expressions from pastors and fellow believers. The intended purpose is to show love and prayer concern to the hurting heart. Therapy, counsel, and other forms of psychological relief are found on the advanced end of the pastoral response.

Undoubtedly, countless believers find the warmth and love necessary to latch onto forward traction within life following the crisis through the pastoral response. Moreover, this response is indispensable and has its proper place in assisting people in finding comfort within a circle of caring believers during times of pain. Therefore, the pastoral response is crucial for supporting counsel within the faith community. Further, the community's love and support are priceless in the face of suffering.

However, there are encounters of suffering salvation when a believer necessitates a theological response. The theological response to suffering salvation seeks to address the moment of pain through the lens of a logical answer extracted from scripture. This response calls upon critical understanding, reflection, and theological observation. The theological response dares to ask challenging questions and seeks discernable outcomes in the form of comprehension. While many believers are content with the comfort of intercessory prayer and a listening ear, others require a logical exegetical answer to their pain.

The theological response is not concerned with a disgraceful demand for an answer for suffering. It is not demanding an answer from God, resembling an entitled mentality. Instead, it is a desire for theological reflection and perception. It is the search for examination and observation. In as much, some believers desire to comprehend why the moment of suffering salvation occurred within their lives. Numerous believers search for meaning and purpose to the pain and misery experienced in their life chapter of suffering salvation. Thus, the theological response prods beyond emotional comfort seeking contemplation for understanding and articulation.

My journey into the Word of God seeking a theological response to suffering salvation was enlightening. Meanwhile, I uncovered that suffering is not an innovative topic in theological discovery. Multitudes of books have been penned concerning the matter. Brilliant theologians throughout history have deliberated and investigated the question at hand.

However, I was yearning within my aching heart to discover what God would reveal to me from His Word concerning suffering salvation. What I uncovered along my journey is the fact that God offers no singular simplistic solution. Herein is a spoiler alert early within this book; absent in the Bible is a one-line zinger to the problem of trials and suffering. Accordingly, this book is void of a nutshell solution to the age-old question at hand. In contrast, I discovered through the study of the Word that the answer to suffering salvation truly is situational.

Moreover, to my surprise, during my season of study, through heartache and pain, I uncovered that the Bible, which is God's authoritative self-disclosure, reveals various examples of suffering salvation within the lives of biblical believers, all of which transpire for a host of assorted reasons. In place of a one-line answer to suffering providing a simplistic solution, the Bible presents a multi-narrative of varying explanations for suffering salvation due to assorted circumstances. Thus, the varying examples of differing reasons for suffering salvation located in the Bible present the argument that the traditional pattern of a singular chosen category of explanation for suffering is flawed.

In other words, this book will argue that believers must abandon the idea of offering one reason for suffering salvation in a broad-brush stroke fashion. Suffering salvation cannot be generalized. For example, preachers informing hurting believers that all suffering occurs due to sin is faulty theology. Preachers and authors must resign the concept of granting the hurting heart a simplistic one-category response for the divine allowance of pain. When asked the question of why God allows suffering salvation, the common response from Christians is one-dimensional. People frequently grant counsel for suffering based upon one example in the Bible. Conversely, the Bible presents a multi-narrative of differing potential reasons, outlined in greater detail throughout this book.

Further, the notion that there is no answer for the permission of suffering salvation also falls short of biblical understanding. Many preachers have emphatically declared that there is no answer for suffering. Numerous articles surmise suffering as being answerless. However, this is not true in every circumstance of suffering. The Bible does, in fact, reveal potential answers to suffering salvation which occur for different reasons.

Does faith matter in terms of suffering salvation? Is a lack of faith always the reason for suffering? What about the fiery trial? The reality of fiery trials, for instance, cannot be denied. However, is it biblical for believers to apply the aspect of the fiery trial as a default template in response to all circumstances of suffering? Free will is an undeniable factor, but what about the sovereignty of God?

Thus, in place of a bullet point simplistic answer, the Bible hosts a multi-array of fluctuating possibilities for suffering salvation depending on the specific situation. Why does God allow suffering salvation? The answer to the provoking question is dependent upon the circumstances. In other words, the answer to why God permits believers to encounter suffering salvation is as follows: It depends.

The theological approach of casting blame upon believers for lack of faith concerning each moment of suffering salvation should be ceased. Likewise, the oversimplified solvent of blaming each experience of suffering salvation upon the devil and spiritual warfare must be removed from the theological response. Blaming the devil for all accounts of suffering is one-dimensional and erroneous.

In as much, personal accountability and consequences of action are not always the source of suffering. In contrast, a holistic and multi-dimensional exploration considering a wide variety of explanations dependent upon the situation at hand must replace the one-track thinking concerning suffering. Consequently, the cause of suffering salvation is as follows: It depends.

Meanwhile, a traditional line of expression echoed by believers within church circles must be abolished early in this book. It is not blasphemy to question God during periods of pain. Scores of believers are suppressed from uncovering a theological response to their pain due to the retort of the faithful casting guilt for the questioning of God. As a lead pastor, I cannot recall the accurate number of moments in which I have heard people shout: You do not question God! However, this is poor counsel absent of foundational biblical merit.

For instance, the disciples carried questions to Jesus when they perceived that His words failed to manifest in truth. However, Jesus simply answered their question in place of scolding them for the inquiry,

> "Then the disciples came to Jesus in private and asked, Why couldn't we drive it out? He replied, Because you have so little faith. Truly I tell you, if you have faith as small as a mustard seed, you can say to this mountain, Move from here to there, and it will move. Nothing will be impossible for you" (Matthew 17:19-21).

Notice that in this narrative, Jesus simply answered their question while adding exhortation, absent of any demonstration of offense. Similarly, it is biblically accurate to recall that God replied to Job with rhetorical prodding in response to Job's questioning during suffering, as will be addressed in chapter 3 of this book (Job 38:4-7).

Conversely, God applied rhetorical questioning in that passage to teach Job a divine principle. Overall, a believer seeking a theological understanding while maintaining a disposition of love, respect, and reverence toward God concerning their moment of suffering salvation is not demonstrating a spirit of rebellion. Simply put, asking God why suffering salvation was permitted reverently is acceptable. God can handle honest questions from loving people.

In the following chapters, I invite you to partake in this journey as I divulge my discovery concerning answers to the dilemma of suffering salvation. I will disclose in this journey six diverse explanations from the Word of God, offering potential comprehension concerning why believers encounter seasons of suffering salvation. As I will reveal, the reason for suffering salvation can often vary greatly depending on a multiplicity of situations and circumstances. There is no one-size-fits-all answer for suffering salvation. Moreover, each of the six explanations shared within this book can be appropriately applied to numerous conditions experienced in the believer's life, all of which may serve to offer theological insight into the reasons for suffering.

The journey presented within this book will then transition into an opportunity for an honest self-examination concerning your experience of suffering salvation, followed by final thoughts regarding suffering combined with a chance for healing and restoration of the inner hurting heart. Suffering salvation frequently levels the recipient with the emotional turmoil that longs for healing and help that Jesus Christ provides. Meanwhile, our journey begins in the ensuing chapter as we delve into the pervasive issue of free will.

Chapter 2
FREE WILL

"But if serving the Lord seems undesirable to you, then choose for yourselves this day whom you will serve, whether the gods your ancestors served beyond the Euphrates or the gods of the Amorites, in whose land you are living. But as for me and my household, we will serve the Lord" (Joshua 24:15).

> Joshua is the fearless leader who followed in the shoes of the renowned leader, Moses. Joshua assumes the responsibility to lead people into righteousness, as well as to lead them into the promise of God. In the midst of this task, he offers his followers' free choice of decision in terms of God. Joshua casts an opportunity of free will before the people; choose for yourself who you will serve. The power of free-will is showcased within this scripture.

Herein is a stark reality concerning assorted moments of suffering salvation: Some suffering directly results from free will choices. To begin with, suffering salvation, in various circumstances, can be the result of the graceful gift of free will. In short, God allows believers to make their own choices regarding action and behavior (Joshua 24:15; John 1:12-13; Proverbs 16:9; John 7:17; 1 Corinthians 10:13; 1 Corinthians 11:1; Ephesians 4:32; James 1:13-16; Isiah 55:6).

Human beings are not mindless machines without the freedom of decision and self-controlled capacities. Lifestyle choices and decisions of action are, in fact, free will behaviors that include the often-unnoticed baggage of aftereffects. God does not make each decision of action on behalf of human beings. Accordingly, even Christians have the power to make personal decisions in life that carry with them the reality of results. Meanwhile, it must be remembered that actions have consequences, however so undesirable.

Nevertheless, a general question looms at this point in the journey into understanding suffering salvation: Why does God fail to intervene and prevent all periods of pain for the believer? One facet of this ambitious examination involves the uninvited impact of free will. The unwelcomed result of God choosing to intervene and prevent all pain for the believer would subtract the ability to make free will choices.

If God, for example, intervened and prevented all heart attacks, humans would then be free to eat in an unhealthy manner and refuse to exercise, absent of any concern. The result would be the removal of action and consequences. The issue of free will grants responsibility to human choice, eradicating the argument that God is to blame for suffering salvation.

A forty-year faithful smoker, believer or non-believer, cannot blame God for developing lung cancer. Meanwhile, a nineteen-year-old who chooses to drive their vehicle under the influence of alcohol cannot blame God for the aftereffects of a collision that kills the opposing driver. Actions have consequences.

On the other side of the coin, scripture does not negate the reality that there are times in life in which believers suffer at the hand of another person's free will. If God intervened and circumvented every murder, accordingly, God would then be nullifying free will. A selfish murderer has free will. A driver under the influence of drugs or alcohol has free will. An abusive spouse has free will. A petty thief has free will. A rapist has free will.

On the contrary, it would be passionately celebrated by humanity if God would proactively prevent all suffering or evil acts. God would be considered a heavenly hero by all reasonable human standards if God chose to inhibit every single act of suffering salvation. God would be elevated to the status of a superhero instantly if all actions of suffering were prevented by divine intervention.

However, doing so would inadvertently handcuff free will. God thwarting every suffering action would strip humanity of the free choice to do good or evil. The ripple effect would undoubtedly undermine the reality of human choice. Likewise, if God, out of love and mercy, intervened and precluded all believers from every form of harm in all situations, God would be effectively robbing humanity of free choice. The sting of this reality is pinching, yet it is reality, nonetheless. Free will is often the answer to numerous circumstances of suffering salvation.

Leaping from the pages of scripture is a transparent record affirming the cause-and-effect of free will. For instance, Adam chose to listen to Eve's plea and succumb to sin, resulting in the fall of humanity (Genesis Chapter 3). However, in no fashion could Adam blame God for his action's negative repercussions. Adam's action was one of free will that brought about the result of sin, causing their eyes to be opened and fallen sin nature to be manifested (Genesis Chapter 3).

In actuality, all of humanity was affected by Adam's free choice and action (Genesis Chapter 3; Romans 5:12; Romans 8:22). God allowed Adam to act upon his free will, and his personal private action affected all humanity in an extraordinarily non-private and non-personal form. The contemporary individualistic culture would decry personal private decisions affecting no one else. Conversely, the decision of Adam gave way to lasting impacts upon all of humanity and even upon the Earth itself (Romans 8:22).

An additional biblical example concerning the effects of free will can be discovered in David by examining his affair with Bathsheba. David chose to have a sexual experience with Bathsheba, which was his private free will action combined with the private free will acceptance of Bathsheba (2 Samuel 11:4). Looking through the standard lens of contemporary individualism, this would be deemed a personal and private steamy affair that failed to affect others. This was indeed David and Bathsheba's personal free will choice. It was a personal-private decision.

However, Bathsheba's husband (Uriah) was ultimately killed due to David's actions (2 Samuel 11:6-15)! Uriah's life was affected and eventually ended due to David's free will actions and decisions following his affair with Bathsheba. Free will in action was the cause of another person's suffering. Uriah's death at the hand of David's decision extends a model concerning the negative impacts of free will on other people's lives. *Free will can affect other people!*

Moving forward, more examples from scripture highlight free will decisions and the counter effects on other people's lives. Even so, consider how Abel was affected by the free will actions of Cain (Genesis 4:8) and how the early church believers were affected by the free will actions of Saul as they were beaten and imprisoned for doing nothing more than passionately following Jesus Christ (Acts 8:1-4). In the same manner, consider how Steven was stoned at the hands of religious leaders operating in free will decision and action (Acts 7:54-60) and how Daniel was cast into a den of lions due to the free will actions of the King (Daniel 6:16). Free will plays a heavy hand in the understanding of suffering salvation. The free will actions of people can, in fact, affect the lives of those around them.

In his well-known work, *Institutes* (1536/1541), John Calvin would disagree as he maintains every action in life to be the direct sovereign command of God. Calvin extends God's role as creator and sustainer to include his absolute control over everything that transpires within the universe, from the most minor action to the most significant action (Calvin, *Institutes* I, Chapter 16). Calvin does not believe that humans possess free will, as God objectively directs all activities, "All events whatsoever are governed by the secret counsel of God" (Calvin, *Institutes* I, Chapter 16). Therefore, Calvin's teaching would eliminate any form of suffering salvation stemming from free will. Further, Calvin denied luck, chance, and coincidence. In the years of scholarship succeeding Calvin, many have clung to this extreme version of God's sovereignty and the lack of free will in human behavioral choice.

The human spirit is indeed bound by sin and unfree before conversion. Correct is Calvin on the notation that the human being is an enslaved person in the spirit to sin, thus unfree, before salvation (John 8:34; Romans 6:6). The human spirit is unfree without Jesus. It is also foundational within theology that the salvation experience, through Christ alone, sets the human spirit free (Romans 6:18). Freedom in Christ is the only true freedom, "So if the Son sets you free, you will be free indeed" (John 8:36). Jesus is true freedom!

Nevertheless, scripture is very transparent concerning the choices of humanity. The Bible calls upon people to choose life (Deuteronomy 30:19), to choose salvation (Joshua 24:15), and to choose to be obedient to God (Isaiah 48:18). The Bible calls upon people to select self-control (2 Timothy 1:7), to choose interpersonal forgiveness (Ephesians 4:32), and to decide to take care of widows and orphans (1 Timothy 5:3-16). Furthermore, the Bible calls upon people to choose to give water to the thirsty (Matthew 10:42), to decide to keep God's commandments (John 14:15), and to choose to be good to others in action as well as in behavior (1 Corinthians 10:24). The power of choice in terms of decision and behavior is evident within scripture.

Jesus proclaims in the Gospel of John a powerful truth concerning the human choice, "Anyone who chooses to do the will of God will find out whether my teaching comes from God or whether I speak on my own" (John 17:17). This passage implies a personal choice. Jesus further states on the matter of human decision, "Then he called the crowd to him along with his disciples and said: "Whoever wants to be my disciple must deny themselves and take up their cross and follow me" (Mark 8:34). This passage, once again, implies a personal choice.

In the same manner, John the Baptist declares, "To all who did receive him, to those who believed in his name, he gave the right to become children of God—children born not of natural descent, nor human decision or a husband's will, but born of God" (John 1:12-13). This passage transparently implies a personal choice. In the book of Revelation, Jesus declares, "Here I am! I stand at the door and knock. If anyone hears my voice and opens the door, I will come in and eat with that person, and they with me" (Revelation 3:20). This passage implies a personal choice of invitation cast unto all who desire to receive.

It is not within the scope of this chapter to offer a theological treatise serving as a counterargument to Calvin or any other doctrine concerning free will. However, the Bible is transparent that people have free will regarding the choice of worship, obedience, action, and the responsibility of reaction and results due to decisions. Sin is the matter at hand. Sin corrupts human thinking and decision making resulting in adverse effects upon self and others. Sin must not be discarded in the discussion of suffering salvation.

The fall of sin within humanity has marred decisions resulting in undesirable reactions, "For the wages of sin is death, but the free gift of God is eternal life in Christ Jesus our Lord" (Romans 6:23 ESV). In a closer examination of this verse, the word for "wages" in the Greek is defined as a ration or pay (Strong's, 1890, G3800). In other words, the word in this text describes getting what is deserved for the action sowed. Thus, sin is often the catalyst for the reaction encountered from free will choices.

The powerful effect that sin and the fall of humankind have had upon the world must be underscored. Even creation itself has been affected by the corruption of sin (Romans 8:22). Paul makes this palpable as he states,

> "That the creation itself will be set free from its bondage to corruption and obtain the freedom of

the glory of the children of God. For we know that the whole creation has been groaning together in the pains of childbirth until now" (Romans 8:21-22 ESV).

Sin has leveled an adverse effect on everything experienced in life. Accordingly, sin has twisted the minds and hearts of people. Sin is a root cause of bad decisions and actions. Paul even goes so far as to say that the minds of unbelievers are blinded (2 Corinthians 4:4). However, God does not remove the freedom of choice from humanity, leaving people blinded with the power to make selfish and hurtful free will decisions.

As a lead pastor and researcher, I adhere to the biblical understanding that humans have the free choice and responsibility of action and reaction. This theological stance can be supported by many patristic period scholars, such as John Chrysostom, the bishop of Constantinople (Hall, 2002, p. 160). I will disclose more from Chrysostom during our journey in understanding suffering salvation within chapter 3.

However, in terms of the topic of free will, Chrysostom affirms the stand as he states, "We are free and masters of our own free choice" (Hall, 2002, p. 163). Chrysostom further casts a contribution to the issue of choice and suffering as he states, "The problem is that human disposition and choice are corrupted by sin [resulting in suffering]" (Hall, 2002, p. 163). Sin is the ultimate source of suffering!

Chrysostom teaches that human disposition and choice are corrupted by sin, often resulting in pain and suffering (Hall, 2002, p, 163). Therefore, suffering salvation is brought about by free will actions and decisions at times and in various circumstances. Therefore, believers must accept the position that suffering salvation, in a variety of moments, befalls at the hands of human choice.

Contributing affirmation to the argument of free will from Chrysostom, patristic period church father Irenaeus draws attention to the words of Jesus in Matthew 23:37, in which he sadly laments over Jerusalem: "How often I have desired to gather your children together as a hen gathers her brood under her wings, and you were not willing" (Hall, 2002, p. 124). Note that Jesus underscores people's lack of choice and willingness in this passage. Irenaeus furthers the claim for free will as he states, "God has placed the power of choice in both human beings as well as angels, so that those who had yielded obedience might justly possess what is good, given indeed by God, but preserved by themselves" (Hall, 2002, p. 124).

God is omnipotent. God has the unlimited ability to do all things that do not conflict with God's own will or nature (McKim, 1996, p. 117). In other words, God is all-powerful! However, God's ability to do all things does not equate to God choosing to do all things. *Take a moment and capture that preceding comment!* Just because God can do everything does not mean God always will. God can intervene and prevent all periods of pain, but that does not mean God always will intervene and stop all periods of pain.

Going further, the omnipotence of God does not eradicate the free choice of human action. Accordingly, if God intervened and circumvented all destructive human activity, free will would be eliminated with certainty. Irenaeus concurs with this argument as he stands upon the theology of human choice stating in brief, "When human beings choose to disobey God, they forfeit what is good, with no small amount of injury and mischief. The results are sad. Still, a human being is in his own power with respect to faith" (Hall, 2002, p. 125). In other words, Irenaeus is saying that humans have the choice to do good or evil, irrespective of how sad the outcome may be within the course of life.

God is not evil. In contrast, God is love (1 John 4:7-21). God never acts in a fashion that is evil (James 1:13-18). God does not do evil acts. In addition, God is not evil simply because God allows evil while possessing the omnipotence to cease all evil. Instead, God is loving and gracious enough to allow humanity to maintain the gift of free will. Nonetheless, for free will to be free will in actuality and not merely in theory, God must willingly permit heartbreaking actions to both God and others.

Closely related, some believers, on various occasions, do not see God's help and protection within their lives because they fail to ask for it; the Bible says that we have not because we ask not (James 4:2-3). The passive decision to not ask for God's help until after suffering salvation manifests is free will in action. Believers cannot blame God if this is the case in life. In other words, the lack of asking for God's help in life is a free will decision that may manifest in periods of suffering. Further, some believers do not see God's protection due to ignorance of God's principles and poor choices (Hosea 4:6). Once again, this is free will in action; believers cannot impute God if this is the case.

Consequently, some believers decide to ignore God's Word and go it alone. The Bible teaches that believers would live in peace if they only would use their free will and be obedient to God (Isaiah 48:18). This is free will in action; believers cannot impugn God if this is the case. Personal choice and decision of action have consequences. Accordingly, some examples of suffering salvation are the more significant result of free will.

More troubling, however, is when a believer is the victim of interpersonal free will decisions. When someone else's decision or behavior presents suffering upon innocent victims, it rings of unfairness in terms of understanding suffering salvation. In contrast, consider the perspective that God intervenes and prevents believers from much unknown harm throughout life (Psalm 91:3-7; Luke 22:31-34; John 10:10). On the other hand, for free will to remain, there must be various instances in which God abstains from intervention. Although the reasoning can be situational, the potential rationale for the absence of God's intervention will continue to be unpacked throughout each lens of possibility presented within this book.

Borrowing from the apostle Paul, the ancient diatribe style of writing (Greathouse, 2008, p. 110): What then? Are we mere victims of our own free will or to the free will of others? God forbid! Believers occupy the ability to make good choices. Positive choices can erode the potential of adverse outcomes eliminating the aspect of being a victim to one's self-will. Additionally, believers can ask for God's wisdom (Jerimiah 33:3) and God's leading within life choices (James 1:5). Believers can ask for God's guidance every day in life and upon their actions (Isiah 58:11; John 14:26).

In terms of being a victim of the results of interpersonal free will, believers can call upon God for help in times of trouble (Psalm 50:15; Psalm 91:15), believers can ask for and claim the protection of God in their daily lives (Psalm 34:7-9), and believers can trust that God is an ever-present help in all circumstances (Psalm 46:1)!

Closely related, believers can walk in the freedom that Jesus grants to experience life covered in God's protection, absent of fear. The prophet Isaiah elevates faith and the promise of God to the believer as he declares the word of God, "Fear not, for I am with you; be not dismayed, for I am your God; I will strengthen you, I will help you, I will uphold you with my righteous right hand" (Isaiah 41:10 ESV).

Moreover, the Bible teaches that God's perfect love drives out fear, "There is no fear in love, but perfect love casts out fear. For fear has to do with punishment, and whoever fears has not been perfected in love" (1 John 4:18 ESV). The word that the writer of 1 John employs for fear in the Greek is *Phobos* meaning: fright, alarm, dread, to be afraid (Strong's, 1890, G5401). Thus, the Word of God exhorts believers to be secured within God's love and removed from fear and fright.

The heart of my journey into understanding suffering salvation disclosed within this book persistently confronts the biblical concept that varying circumstances can contribute to suffering salvation due to differing details; there is no one-size-fits-all answer to suffering in the Bible. Equally, the subsequent question remains in direct response to our discussion concerning free will: Is every moment of suffering salvation the result of free will? No.

However, are selected accounts of suffering salvation the direct result of free will? Yes. Are various instances of physical illness and suffering brought on by free will decisions and individual human choice? Yes. Can it be said that various occurrences of tragedies transpire as the result of free will? Yes. Choices and decisions are often the root cause of suffering and pain. Personal self-afflicted decisions of free will can explain suffering salvation in specific occurrences and circumstances. Likewise, suffering salvation can also, in various moments, befall due to free will in the interpersonal form.

Nonetheless, can a doctrine concerning suffering salvation be established, concluding that free will is the end sum of the matter? No. Imputing every occurrence that serves to be unfortunate upon the free actions and behaviors of human beings is misplaced theology. Do scores of believers suffer due to humans choosing to sin and act out in selfish forms? Yes. Free will would be exterminated if God prevented each negative event, resulting in a drastically different human experience.

Conversely, not every instance of suffering salvation results from free will. Making such an accusation leads to unfortunate insight and poor counsel. Yet, various accounts of suffering salvation must rest under the umbrella of free will. Overall, the answer to why believers experience suffering salvation is as follows: It depends.

In the following chapter, our journey into understanding suffering salvation continues as we peer into the omniscient nature of God's incomprehensible understanding.

Chapter 3
THE BIG PICTURE

> *"Where were you when I laid the earth's foundation? Tell me if you understand. Who marked off its dimensions? Surely you know! Who stretched a measuring line across it? Have you comprehended the vast expanses of the earth? Tell me if you know all this"* (Job 38:4-5; 18-19).

> In what is believed to be the oldest book written within the canon of scripture, Job had many questions for God concerning his insufferable suffering. In turn, God made His point transparent with a host of rhetorical replies intended to produce humility. The result from scripture is the big picture view of God versus the limited view of humanity.

A sportsman deep within the woods on a brisk fall morning traversing through the colorful fallen crisp autumn leaves will fail to see the forest's big picture due to the trees' viewpoint. Likewise, the poor vision of the temporary often blurs the big picture. In the same manner, God's knowledge supersedes the limited human view of understanding. God sees the forest of life, while humans are often limited to the view of the trees.

God is unlimited. Nothing is hidden from God (Proverbs 15:3). God sees the end from the beginning (1 John 3:20). God is infinite. God is divine. Furthermore, God is the immortal and invisible King of ages who dwells in unapproachable light (1 Timothy 1:17; 1 Timothy 6:16). God is not an ontologically limited human. Instead, God is an incorporeal Spirit containing all wisdom, power, glory, majesty, authority, and dominion (John 4:24; Jude 1:25). In such, God has foreknowledge of all events past, present, and future (Psalm 147:5).

Even more, God comprehends every trivial detail concerning the complexities of all potential events that failed ever to transpire. Within the deity of the one true living God is contained infinite knowledge of every detail concerning humanity, the universe, human choice, the cascading countereffects of human will, possibilities, outcomes, and potential outcomes. The prophet Isaiah says it best as he says, "Do you not know? Have you not heard? The Lord is the everlasting God, the Creator of the ends of the earth. He will not grow tired or weary, and his understanding no one can fathom" (Isiah 40:28).

God is omniscient. God knows all things and circumstances perfectly and immediately (McKim, 1996, p. 117). The ability to understand God is incomprehensible to humanity. Isaiah humbly sums up this idea, "For my thoughts are not your thoughts, neither are your ways my ways, declares the Lord. As the heavens are higher than the earth, so are my ways higher than your ways and my thoughts than your thoughts" (Isiah 55:8-9).

Ludicrous is the thought process that humans know greater than God. What seems to make sense to the wisdom or understanding of humanity pales in comparison to God's reasoning and decision process. The apostle Paul makes this discernable as he states, "For the wisdom of this world is foolishness in God's sight" (1 Corinthians 3:19). Human wisdom is foolishness compared to God's wisdom. Human understanding falls short in the light of God's knowledge.

Humans, unlike God, have the disadvantage of inadequate information concerning the big picture of life and events. Humans are not divine. Humans are limited. Humans are physical. Humans are not omnipresent and omniscient. Humans are finite. Humans do not know the end from the beginning. Humans are incomplete in their perception of all things. Humanity does not have foreknowledge of all events past, present, and future. Humans do not contain the capacity to comprehend every trivial detail concerning the complexities of all events and potential events that failed ever to transpire.

A biblical example of this can be discovered in the garden narrative. When Jesus was attacked in the garden, this did not make sense to Peter. Accordingly, Peter took control of the seemingly senseless situation and cut an ear off in defense, only to find Jesus rebuking him for not comprehending the moment (John 18:10-12). Humans are limited to the scope of understanding and are bound by time and reason. What did not make sense to Peter was understood by Jesus.

In this situation, humanity could not see beyond the moment, while deity possessed knowledge of the moment and the possible future results. In other words, the example of Peter's failure to comprehend the moment serves as a prime model of our misunderstanding, in various situations, of suffering salvation. Like Peter, believers often misunderstand why God allows differing encounters of suffering salvation.

Believers are emotionally broken, at times, due to their failure to fathom what God already understands. *Take a moment to absorb the preceding comment!* Our pain, while often not cognized, is fully realized by God. We are shortsighted. We are emotional beings driven by what we see, feel, taste, think, and can touch. God, in contrast, is a non-changing Spirit (John 4:24; Malachi 3:6; Hebrews 13:8) who moves and speaks based upon infinite knowledge. We view most events through the temporary lens, while God views all events through the lens of eternity. In other words, God understands what we fail to understand. Thus, God permits suffering salvation, at times, for reasons beyond the limited human discernment.

To illustrate and teach the idea presented, allow some poignant metaphors to highlight the construct: Consider the confused domestic cat undergoing realignment, permitted by its owners, of a broken leg. The cat fails to comprehend why the owner voluntarily permits the veterinarian to inflict the pain of realignment. Any pet owner in a similar scenario can testify that the animal will strike in defense and cry out in confounded agony.

The lack of big-picture comprehension is the product of failed momentary misunderstandings. Indeed, humans are not cats, as humans possess a more advanced level of intellect. However, the point of articulation in context is founded upon the understanding that humans have a limited scope of comprehension compared to the unlimited God.

On the same side of the coin, visualize the mindset of a six-month-old baby on vaccine day. The baby is carried into a bright room and is stripped down to the diaper. The parent then lays the baby on a firm and foreign table, all while allowing a giant, towering stranger to stab them with a needle. The baby screams out, confused in pain.

Contemplate this scenario for a moment if you would. It would be fair to suggest that the baby could think if they possessed the cognitive ability, the following questions: Why is my parent allowing this mean stranger to stab me? Does my parent not care about my pain? Why is my pain being permitted? The answers to the above rhetorical metaphoric questions bring to the surface the palpable fact that the parent knows what is best even though the baby does not contain the compacity to comprehend the moment.

Like the above examples, believers are limited in compacity to comprehend why God chooses to allow suffering salvation throughout various moments within life. However, failing to understand why the unlimited all-knowing God, who knows all faculties and details concerning the big picture of eternity, allows evil or heartbreaking moments to transpire absent of His intervention does not grant permission to distrust God. There will be moments in which God permits periods of pain that supersede human understanding.

As I referenced in chapter 2, John Chrysostom was the bishop of Constantinople and is remembered today as one of the greatest patristic period preachers (Hall, 2002, p. 160; Christianity Today, n.d., para. 13). On the issue of suffering and the allowance of evil, he states, "Whatsoever God does, He does so out of His exceeding great care and kindness" (Young, 2017, para. 8). Chrysostom consistently denies that human evil is the result of God's action (Hall, 2002, p. 162). God is not an evil spirit, and God does not perform acts of evil. Likewise, it is not logical to deduce God as evil in nature because He permits suffering salvation.

Moreover, God's understanding is beyond measure (Psalm

147:5). Coupled with God's knowledge is the reality that God's goodness is well established (Exodus 34:6; Psalm 31:19; Psalm 107:1; Psalm 145:9; Nahum 1:7; Mark 10:18; James 1:17; 1 John 4:8). In various moments over the span of life believers are the proverbial confused baby, and God simply contains greater understanding concerning the permitted period of pain. Therefore, multiple moments of miscomprehension over suffering salvation result from fallible limited humans not comprehending what the infallible, unlimited, all-knowing God identifies.

Writing in powerful metaphor, the apostle Paul speaks to the reality concerning the limited understanding of humanity as he states,

> "For we know in part, and we prophesy in part, but when completeness comes, what is in part disappears. When I was a child, I talked like a child, I thought like a child, I reasoned like a child. When I became a man, I put the ways of childhood behind me. For now, we see only a reflection as in a mirror; then we shall see face to face. Now I know in part; then I shall know fully, even as I am fully known" (1 Corinthians 13:9-12).

Humans, in this world bound by the restrictions of fallen nature, are limited in knowledge, while God holds full knowledge. One of the glories of Heaven will be the increase in comprehension as the dimmed light of inadequate human reasoning is removed. Yet, living in this world bound by the darkness of limitation will give way to moments in which a lack of understanding will demand the trust of the unlimited God of glory. Suffering salvation, in various situations, can be explained as being the more significant result of God understanding what believers fail to discern.

However, much intrapersonal conflict arises in the misfire between the human comprehension of the divine perfection along the crossroads of suffering salvation. Please make note that intrapersonal conflict varies from interpersonal conflict. Interpersonal conflict is an interruption of a relationship between two or more people (Britannica, 2014, para. 1). Interpersonal conflict arises when the ideas, beliefs, opinions, or desires between two or more people erupt into a fracture or hindrance within the relationship.

Interpersonal conflict, therefore, is the incongruity of motives or desires between two or more individuals. Various conflicts can be positive, helpful, and settled in a healthy fashion. However, other conflicts can become destructive and detrimental to the unity of relationships, organizations, or churches (Cox, 2020, p. 33).

Conversely, intrapersonal conflict rages within as it is conflict within self. Intrapersonal conflict is an internal dispute arising from a person's thoughts, emotions, expectations, or ideas. Additionally, intrapersonal conflict can involve internal emotional/psychological conflict against God. This is due, in large part, to the fact that believers often become emotionally broken and angry when failure to understand why suffering salvation occurs. We like to be in control of our circumstances; a loss of control often breeds anger and hurt.

Even so, a lack of control is often so unsettling that anger becomes directed upward. When we fail to comprehend why something is happening, we quickly grow angry, casting blame upon a source perceived to have held the ability to intervene. Sources of higher power are frequently viewed as responsible for acting on behalf of those with less power. For instance, when a murder occurs, community members jump as fast as lightning to whip the tongue, asking: Where were the police? When a loved one is diagnosed with incurable cancer, the most apparent knee-jerk reaction is to place a demand upon the medical community, asking: Cannot the doctor do something to help?

Moreover, when a child accidentally drowns in a lake, the media often spurts out in immediate haste, asking: Did not the parent or guardian attempt to save the child? Humans hold a tendency to expect higher powers to solve situations. In as much, frequent blame is cast upon the perceived source of an authority having the power to prevent the pain.

In psychology scholarship, this can be understood as a defense mechanism known as the fallacy of fairness. In general, defense mechanisms are unconscious psychological responses that protect people from feelings of anxiety, threats to self-esteem, and things that they do not want to think about or deal with (Cherry, 2021, para. 1). First described by Sigmund Freud in his psychoanalytic theory, defense mechanisms function to protect against anxiety. Several manifest within human behavior (Cherry, 2021, para. 1). Virtually commonplace in all human conduct, defense mechanisms are a fact of life.

Meanwhile, in the mechanism of the fallacy of fairness, there is a misplaced yearning of desire for equal treatment decrying unfairness for perceived suffering. This is further explained as the suffering person anticipates that the other person (the highest source) should know their needs and respond to them appropriately

(Ledden, 2018, para. 14). In this defense mechanism, there is a complete disavowal of responsibility or communication. Often the blamer seeks the moral high ground (Ledden, 2018, para. 14). Moral high ground or moral displacement is equally a factor within this aspect of internal crisis or anxiety.

The fallacy of fairness or even moral high ground displacement are both genuine responses often found within the case of suffering salvation. Understood simply, a failure of comprehension conjoined with a loss of control often generates anger toward God. While this response may be subconscious and unintentional, it is frequent.

To further comprehend the fallacy of fairness, human society is governed by conventions and rules – they are called laws and regulations in the study of psychology. These are black-and-white, cut-and-dry rules and regulations in a given culture (Therapy Now SF, 2021, para 2). This being the common psychological stance, the fallacy of fairness arises when an individual attempts to apply similar rules to interactions with people in their personal life (Therapy Now SF, 2021, para. 2).

In other words, the suffering person often perceives unfairness casting blame upon higher positions of authority when accepted conventional rules appear to be overruled. There is always a perceived unfairness when something goes someone else's way; fairness is not objective but subjective (Therapy Now SF, 2021, para. 3).

This being the case, a believer in Christ who has a cultivated relationship with God looks unto God as the highest source of power, hope, help, healing, and intervention. Thus, when the highest power (God) fails to display said power in the act of intervention concerning suffering salvation, anger and bitterness toward God often follow suit. The idea of God holding all power and ability is solid theology, as Jesus declares He has all power and authority in heaven and on Earth (Matthew 28:18).

Moreover, when a believer has an experience of suffering salvation absent of the perceived intervention of God, anger toward God is often the result. Given that God holds the highest authority, there is frequently a sense of belief that God has been passive when the believer was in need concerning a moment suffering salvation. In other words, God gets a bad rap when Christians suffer.

A biblical example of this internal emotional letdown can be discovered as Mary and Martha lament while informing Jesus that his passive absence contributed to their brother's death, "Lord, Martha said to Jesus, if you had been here, my brother would not have died" (John 11:22). The passage of Jesus raising Lazarus from the dead is often considered to be the climax of signs within the gospel of John elevating Jesus as a life giver and miracle worker. Yet, before this climaxing moment of life returning into a dead man's body, Jesus is blamed for passivity. Stones could be cast at Martha for her statement toward Jesus.

However, her words unto Jesus reflect her emotional letdown as she perceived apathy and passiveness demonstrated by the highest of all powers. It could be suggested from the narrative that Martha is showing the defensive mechanism of the fallacy of fairness or even moral ground displacement based upon her casting blame upon the highest authority (God). Martha does not utter this quivering question in isolation. Multitudes of believers have echoed the same inquiry unto God during moments of suffering salvation.

Failure to understand why the omnipotent (all-powerful)

and omniscient (all-knowing) God fails to intervene does not justify a failure to believe. We are limited in understanding. God, in contrast, is unlimited in knowledge. We must maintain a solid conviction that the omniscient (all-knowing) God of the universe knows more concerning the actions and interactions of divine assistance than we know. God understands all possibilities, complexities, and all results of actions, as well as all possible consequences of his interactions (Isaiah 46:10; Isaih 55:8-13). Suffering salvation being permitted to unfold, in various moments, directly results from God knowing the big picture.

Faith, in contrast, requires believers to relinquish control and invest trust in the goodness of God in all situations. This suggests that moments will occur in our walk with God when sorrowful situations result in a loss of control and a lack of understanding. Moreover, faith that is strong enough to move mountains is not impervious to circumstances where trust must replace comprehension.

However, failure to grasp why the infinite God, in His omniscience, does not interfere when deemed best by believers demands the trust of God. We must trust that God is good (1 Chronicles 16:34) and that God is love (1 John 4:16). In the same way, we must trust that God is merciful (Deuteronomy 4:31) and that God has good plans for our lives (Jerimiah 29:11). Nonetheless, various encounters of suffering salvation may remain clouded by the partial understanding of limited human cognition until the veil is removed in eternity (1 Corinthians 13:12).

Returning to the early wisdom of John Chrysostom, he shares that even the patristic period church fathers wrestled with the difficulty of reconciling divine providence and human suffering. However, Chrysostom suggests that perspective contributes to understanding as he says, "It is not so much events themselves, but how we view them, through what lens and with what disposition, that will make the difference" (Hall, 2002, p. 161). The reconciliation of suffering salvation with God's omnipotence (all-powerful nature) is mysterious and challenging.

Conversely, humanity is flawed and limited in the knowledge of all things past, present, and future, influencing the emotional bearing of suffering situations. Is this book arguing that all moments of suffering salvation result from God knowing the big picture? No. Conversely, are various circumstances of suffering salvation the more significant result of God permitting pain due to understanding the big picture? Yes.

The core of my journey into suffering salvation unveiled within this book untiringly encounters the biblical concept that varying circumstances can contribute to suffering salvation due to differing details. There is no one-size-fits-all answer to suffering in the Bible. Why God allows believers to experience suffering salvation is a broad pervasive question that cannot be answered with a single swipe upon the canvas of life. Instead, this book attempts to provide a theological response through the vein of a line-by-line scalpel approach. Each moment of suffering salvation contains its own unique set of situational circumstances.

Equally, the subsequent question remains in direct response to our discussion concerning the omniscience of God: Is each experience of suffering salvation the result of God knowing the big picture? No. On the other hand, are selected moments of suffering salvation the direct result of God's permissive allowance due to God knowing the big picture? Yes. Are various instances of physical illness and traumatic suffering permitted by God, irrespective of our faith and obedience? Yes.

In the meantime, can we state with certainty that all matters of suffering salvation directly result from God knowing the big picture with zero blame and responsibility being leveled upon our actions or lack of displayed faith? No. Attributing each instance that is unfortunate to the permission of God's omniscience is erroneous theology. Moreover, making such an assumption advances anger and frustration toward a good and loving God while removing personal accountability of free will, faith, and knowledge of scripture. For this reason, not every moment of suffering salvation can be leveled upon the omniscience of God.

Conversely, there remain mysterious moments of suffering salvation that fail to be redeemed by any form of comprehensible recognition. In these painful periods, believers must take a page from Chrysostom and view the unfortunate event through the lens of a loving God who knows the end from the beginning (Hall, 2002, p. 161). Overall, the answer to why believers experience suffering salvation is as follows: It depends.

In the following chapter, our journey into understanding suffering salvation continues as we explore the dynamic perspective of faith.

Chapter 4
THE FAITH FACTOR

"He [Jesus] could not do any miracles there, except lay his hands on a few sick people and heal them. He was amazed at their lack of faith" (Mark 6:5-6).

> The gospel of Mark is the shortest of all four of the Gospels, yet it is considered to be the original or first written. In this work, Jesus reportedly did not do many miracles in his hometown of Nazareth due to a lack of faith within the people. As water slowly absorbs into dry thirsty soil, allow this reality to sink into the heart: Jesus was limited in the realm of the miraculous, in various circumstances, due to a lack of faith.

At this moment in our journey to understanding suffering salvation, the cat must be let out of the proverbial bag. Some experiences of suffering salvation directly result from a lack of faith. There it is out in the open! It has been stated transparently. It is true that faith matters in the realm of divine intervention. The issue of faith cannot be sidestepped when grappling with suffering, as convenient as that maneuver may be to the emotions. Perhaps this may be a difficult pill to swallow.

However, suppose this book is going to address the truth in terms of suffering salvation. In that case, it must be underscored that there are various situations in which suffering salvation occurs within the lives of believers due to a lack of faith. Faith moves God. Faith matters in the lives of believers. Faith cannot be excused.

Diving into the matter at hand, the Bible does not take kindly to followers of Christ who fail to walk in fortified faith. Believers are directed, in the Word of God, to build and maintain strong faith. For instance, Jesus rebuked His disciples for displaying a lack of faith during a storm (Mark 4:35-41). Moreover, multiple times Jesus is found uttering the infamous rebuke in terms of faith, which remains a popularly quoted biblical phrase in modern culture, "You of little faith" (Matthew 6:30; Matthew 8:26; Matthew 16:18; Luke 12:28). How many times have you heard someone quote those words from Jesus? Faith is elevated in these texts as paramount within the interaction of God. Faith is important.

Furthermore, Jesus taught that believers are to have faith in order to see the miraculous divine interaction of God, "Therefore I tell you, whatever you ask for in prayer, believe that you have received it, and it will be yours" (Mark 11:24). Herein is a direct textual example stating that believers are to ask in faith prior to receiving. Subsequent is the promise of a faith-answered prayer. A more profound unpacking of faith will be provided later in this chapter. Conversely, Jesus transparently teaches faith as fundamental. Faith matters in the lives of believers.

In terms of the importance of faith, Jesus opens wide the window of possibilities within the lives of believers when He states that all things are possible for the person who believes (Mark 9:23). Jesus says that all things, not little things, are possible to those who believe. This strikes counter to those who display weak faith. Within the scope of "all things" is room for belief in the miraculous intervention of God.

According to Jesus, strong faith, being opposed to weak faith, creates space for unlimited answered prayer. Context and cross-referencing are critical to biblical interpretation. Therefore, these promises must be unpacked in light of the words within the letter of first John concerning faith as the writer says, "This is the confidence we have in approaching God: that if we ask anything according to his will, He hears us" (1 John 5:14). Thus, these passages read in tandem propose understanding that a strong belief in divine abilities and within the specific biblical promises opens the door to God's miraculous activity within the lives of believers.

Likewise, Jesus teaches that faith, even as small as a mustard seed, would be able to speak to mountainous situations and see them removed (Matthew 17:19-20). This principle underscores the importance of faith within the Christian life. Jesus teaches this same concept once again in the book of Matthew, dealing with the fig tree as He says,

> "Truly I tell you, if you have faith and do not doubt, not only can you do what was done to the fig tree, but also you can say to this mountain, 'Go, throw yourself into the sea,' and it will be done. If you believe, you will receive whatever you ask for in prayer" (Matthew 21:21-22).

Strong faith is displayed within this passage. Jesus teaches that the believer is to stand in faith, and limitless will be the proceeding possibilities. Is it clear that faith matters in terms of God interacting with people?

Moreover, when healing the infamous woman with the issue of blood, Jesus tells her that her faith has made her well (Matthew 9:22). Notice that when He speaks to her, faith is underscored at the moment as being the single primary factor within the divine intervention equation. Faith is highlighted in the human-divine interaction in this narrative (Matthew 9:22). In the same manner, when Jesus was dealing with the nameless man bound with leprosy, following the act of healing, Jesus tells him that it was his faith that made him well (Luke 17:19). Once again, faith was a forenamed factor in the healing.

Even so, Jesus healed the infamous blind Bartimaeus due to faith shown forth before the moment of divine interaction. Following the actions of faith displayed by Bartimaeus, Jesus says to him, "Your faith has healed you" (Mark 10:52). Once more, faith was the leading noted factor in the miraculous healing concerning this narrative. Altogether taken within context, a discussion concerning suffering salvation must include the fundamental factor that faith plays in the equation. In various circumstances, suffering salvation can directly result from a lack of faith on the believer's part.

Conversely, faith must first be correctly understood from a biblical perspective to be applied to the discussion of suffering salvation in the proper context. Misplaced context concerning faith often contributes to poor theology regarding suffering salvation. A glance of theological reflection concerning faith can underpin a lush comprehension in the time of reflection upon suffering.

Furthermore, a rich grasp of faith must surpass the substandard versions perpetuated so frequently within contemporary Christianity. Faith is often the victim of drive-by teachings that do the biblical concept a great injustice. When believers use the word faith, multiple is the mountainous amounts of teachings that follow. Thus, our journey into understanding suffering salvation must take the opportunity to provide an accurate examination of faith in terms of how it applies to suffering.

What is faith? To begin with, faith is more significant, for instance, than access to gain. Faith is not a cheap gimmick or a quick manipulative tool employed merely to receive something from God! So often within contemporary Christianity, the word faith is thrown forth as if it is the Christian's version of a get-rich-quick scheme or a device used to draw materialistic goodies from heaven.

Faith is not a measuring stick for materialism or consumeristic desires. Faith is not a heavenly debit card issued by God available for unlimited withdrawal upon request. Faith is not an access card for a divine handout. Faith is not a microwave; more importantly, God is not a divine genie existing to meet our on-demand requests. Faith consists of something weightier than a tool used to acquire possessions from God. Equally, faith supersedes manipulative prayers or demanding preferences in every situation. Faith is not the equivalent of a bourgeois life of selfish gain.

In the same manner, faith is not blind belief or ignorant religion. Faith is not a crutch for the weak or the uneducated. Faith must be fully embraced beyond all the inferior promotions and small conventions. In contrast to the descriptions above, faith is fundamental to the believer's interaction with God, "And without faith it is impossible to please God, because anyone who comes to him must believe that he exists and that he rewards those who earnestly seek him" (Hebrews 11:6). An absence of faith produces a lack of connection with God.

So then, the question concerning faith must be grounded in simplistic biblical truth as it applies to the discernment of suffering salvation. Faith, in the most primary aspect, is trust in God. Faith is an active trust in God. It is a trust in God's promises and God's Word. Faith is trusting that God is and that God can do what the Word says God can do. Faith is trust in God and in the biblical promises of God.

Textual support for this argument is found within scripture. In the Old Testament, the word for faith, in Hebrew, is *Emunah*. Faith in the Old Testament means to be firm (Greathouse, 2008, p. 59). It is used in the Old Testament in the physical sense of being steadfast or faithful (Greathouse, 2008, p. 59). In other words, it applies closely to the English idiomatic statement of holding steady or staying firm (Greathouse, 2008, p. 59). Thus, faith in the Old Testament means to be firm in belief, firm in God, or hold steady in the truth of God.

Meanwhile, the word penned by the New Testament writers for faith is the Greek noun, *Pistis*. This word is defined as persuasion, assurance, or confidence (Strong's, 1890, G4102). For example, the Greek word *Pistis* is employed for faith throughout multiple passages in the New Testament, such as in the following scriptural references: Hebrews 11:1; Hebrews 11:6; Matthew 17:20; Matthew 21:21; Mark 5:34; Luke 5:20, et. al. In fact, *Pistis* is used for faith 238 times in the Bible (Thayer and Smith, 1999). Over and over, *Pistis* is applied in the Bible as meaning trust or confidence in God. Therefore, faith, applied adequately in scripture, means to display trust, reliance, confidence, belief, or assurance in God!

On the other hand, faith is not a tool to be employed in the mere acquisition of materialistic possessions. Instead, faith is an active heartfelt status of trusting that God is whom He says He is, that God can do what He says He can do, and that what the Bible says about God is true. Faith is trusting that God is love. Faith is trusting that God is omnipotent. Faith is trusting that God is omniscient. Faith is trusting that God is omnipresent. Faith is trusting that God can perform His Word. Additionally, faith is trusting that God not only hears the prayer of the Christian but that God will do what He said He would do in the lives of Christians!

For further scriptural affirmation of the claim, the writer of Hebrews gives the fundamental understanding of faith, "Now faith is confidence in what we hope for and assurance about what we do not see" (Hebrews 11:1). The intent of this passage in Hebrews promotes faith as confidence in what we believe concerning God. Thus, faith (*Pistis*) is trust in God. When Jesus, in the Gospels, rebukes people for having weak or little faith, He condemns the lack of trust in God. On the other hand, when Jesus connects a miracle to the variable of faith, He elevates the individual's trust in God.

For instance, when Jesus contributes the healing of the woman with the issue of blood to her faith (*Pistis*), He is stating that it was her trust, assurance, or confidence in God that made her well (Matthew 9:22). Likewise, when Jesus heals blind Bartimaeus, He contributes the miracle to the man's faith. Bartimaeus's trust, assurance, or confidence in God welcomed the touch of divine intervention into his physical situation (Mark 10:46-52).

Moreover, faith is trust in God. Faith is trust that God is not a man that He should lie (Numbers 29:13), that God is fully able to perform His Word (Jeremiah 12), and that God is good on all His promises (Psalm 145:13). Likewise, faith is trust that God can perform miracles (Psalm 77:14), that God can do anything (Philippians 3:21), and that the Word of God is eternally reliable truth (John 17:17).

In addition to faith being recognized as trust, assurance, or confidence in God, faith should sustain the way of life for the believer. Paul affirms this aspect of faith as he states, "For we live by faith, not by sight" (2 Corinthians 5:7). Faith, trust, or confidence in God should not be an occasional position for the believer. Faith for the believer must be the daily intentional pursuit of life. The faith way of life stands in contrast to living by the carnal desires of the world, absent of speaking and believing what the Word of God says over the life of the believer.

The good news is, according to the Bible, all believers possess a measure of faith. Faith exists within all believers. Faith is a gift from God! As a matter of fact, faith is a grace gift from God! Nonexistent is a believer who does not possess faith. This claim is unquestionably well-founded within the scripture. For instance, the apostle Paul says,

> "For I say, through the grace given unto me, to every man that is among you, not to think of himself more highly than he ought to think; but to think soberly, according as God hath dealt to every man the measure of faith" (Romans 12:3).

The Greek word applied within this passage for the word "measure" affirms the presence of faith within each believer, as it is defined as a limited portion or degree (Strong's, 1890, G3358). Accordingly, as a grace gift from God, every believer possesses a limited amount of faith! Faith is not an unequally applied gift.

In fact, if you know Jesus Christ as the savior, there is a measure of faith within you! Hence, the understanding for the believer is transparent as God grants unto every Christian a limited portion of faith. It can be stated from the Bible that every believer has at least a limited portion or degree of faith. Faith is a gift of God's grace that all believers receive. Therefore, no one born again can claim the absence of faith.

Considering the biblical understanding concerning faith, the following question emerges when discussing suffering salvation: How can Jesus rebuke people for lack of faith when all believers possess a measure of faith? The matter at hand is not one of having faith versus not having faith.

In contrast, it is a matter of weak faith versus strong faith. It is a matter of edified faith or developed faith versus faith being permitted to be dormant and weak. The limited portion of faith granted by God to all believers is intended to be strengthened and developed!

Faith is like a muscle within the human body, as it must be developed or strengthened. If faith is not applied, it gets weak. If faith is not developed, it can remain as a limited portion. In the same manner, if faith is not exercised, it remains flabby! Faith must be exercised. Faith must be edified. Faith must be developed. Faith must be elevated to the next level.

Consequently, faith is strengthened or built up by reading and hearing the Word of God, "Faith comes from hearing the message, and the message is heard through the word about Christ" (Romans 10:17). Faith is strengthened by hearing and reading the Word! When the believer reads the Word, faith is strengthened. When the believer listens to the Word preached, faith is strengthened. Are you exercising your faith?

Similarly, faith is strengthened when the believer listens to the Word taught in class or small groups. Faith is strengthened when the believer gathers with other believers for corporate worship, and the songs contain Word-based lyrics. When the believer partakes in Word-based testimonies proclaiming the goodness of God within the lives of others, faith is strengthened.

Faith is strengthened when believers gather to discuss and share the Word through study and fellowship. Therefore, the believer must apply intentional efforts to strengthen faith! If a believer fails to develop their faith, how can they exercise the strong faith necessary to trust God for divine intervention?

Strong faith believes in what the Word says over what the world says. Faith that is strong, developed, and edified by hearing the Word of God, is faith that refuses to live by physical sight (2 Corinthians 5:7). Likewise, strong faith believes and stands upon the promises of God (2 Peter 1:4) and speaks the possibilities of God (Romans 4:17), versus uttering doubt and unbelief based upon the physical eyesight. Strong faith stares staunchly into the face of adversity and trusts God to perform His Word. Even so, strong faith developed and edified by the Word, practices prayer and Bible study out of relationship long before the crisis arrives.

In terms of suffering salvation, faith cannot be excused as an insignificant factor. It is not biblically accurate to suggest that faith never, in any circumstance, has any ingredient in suffering salvation. It is false to assume that faith does not matter. The Bible transparently calls upon believers to develop their faith in God and to be able to stand upon the promises of God. If faith had never played any role in the aspect of divine intervention, then Jesus would have never rebuked people for displaying a lack of faith.

Accordingly, if faith never submits a dynamic in terms of suffering salvation, then Jesus would not have celebrated strong faith in the occasions of healing and miracles. Jesus honored strong trust in God, such as in the case of the woman with the issue of blood (Matthew 9:20-22) and in the healing of Blind Bartimaeus (Mark 10:46-52), which reveals that faith matters in moments of human need. Jesus highlighted when faith was significant in people's lives!

For the believer to deny the importance of solid faith in moments of suffering is to deny the fundamental teaching of faith in scripture. My journey into understanding suffering salvation is bold, candid, and Word-based. Therefore, it is biblical to suggest that various circumstances of suffering salvation unfold void of divine intervention due to a lack of strong faith.

Yes, it must be said that a lack of faith displayed in God can, in various circumstances, result in the absence of divine assistance. If Jesus rebuked people for maintaining a lack of faith in biblical times, then it stands to reason that Jesus still rebukes the lack of faith today (Malachi 3:6; Hebrews 13:8). God is immutable. This means God does not change. Further, the principles of God do not change. God never changes in essence or message.

Thus, if Jesus equated faith as a variable in the miraculous events in human need during biblical times, it is theologically consistent to suggest that Jesus continues to celebrate faith in times of trial today. There is no more accurate and biblically transparent example of this dynamic than Jesus not being able to perform many miracles in his hometown. The Bible reports that Jesus was amazed at their lack of faith (Mark 6:5-6). Jesus, God in the flesh, was hindered in performing miracles due to a lack of human faith.

In review, Jesus teaches believers to maintain faith in God. Faith has been defined from scripture as having trust or confidence in God prior to seeing the need manifest in the natural. Likewise, believers are to ask, receive, and believe in faith long before divine intervention is realized. This is clear from the words of Jesus,

> "Have faith in God. Truly I tell you, if anyone says to this mountain, 'Go, throw yourself into the sea,' and does not doubt in their heart but believes that what they say will happen, it will be done for them. Therefore, I tell you, whatever you ask for in prayer, believe that you have received it, and it will be yours" (Mark 11:22-24).

A lack of trust, asking, and believing can potentially result in the absence of divine action.

The issue of suffering salvation in various circumstances is further compounded by the sobering reality that many people wait to beckon God for help after exploring all other possibilities. In other words, for many, God is the final option, yet the first to receive the blame for poor outcomes. Many reserve prayer to be the last-ditch effort and expect it to work. Scores of believers pray defensively once suffering manifests versus developing faith preventively long before the trouble arrives.

Even worse, others ignore God completely until a crisis unfolds. The crisis is often viewed as an opportune time to pray when in actuality, the believer should cultivate a relationship in prayer long before the crisis develops. It is the idea of ignoring the family until the family's help is needed. While God may grace a person, it is not recommended to ignore God until something is needed *from* God.

Suppose God is being used as a last-minute hookup in the moment of calamity combined with weak faith that has not been developed and strengthened by regular intake of the Word of God. In that case, the result *may* be the absence of divine intervention. Yes, strong faith matters in terms of avoiding suffering salvation. Yes, a cultivated relationship with God matters in terms of preventing suffering salvation. Yes, developed faith matters in terms of suffering salvation.

However, my journey into understanding suffering salvation simultaneously includes exposure to extrabiblical teachings in terms of faith. Teachings on the opposite end of the faith spectrum that suggest all moments of suffering salvation to be forever the result of a lack of strong faith are outrageous and extrabiblical. Yes, various moments of suffering salvation experienced within life can result from a lack of developed faith. In the meantime, it is proportionately not true that every moment of suffering is the result of a lack of developed faith.

The Bible is void of any contextual evidence affirming that every single moment of suffering salvation occurs due to the faith factor. Teachings that cast all blame upon a lack of faith in every circumstance of suffering salvation are erroneous and contribute to unnecessary emotional pain and spiritual damage. Some well-known "faith teachers" will suggest that suffering salvation is always the fault of a lack of faith. These type of faith applications are flawed and biblically inaccurate. Jesus indeed rebukes believers in the Gospels concerning a lack of faith. However, it is not true that all moments of suffering situations are the result of a lack of faith.

For example, the apostle Paul displayed strong faith, yet he still was shipwrecked, beaten with rods, and stoned once by the hands of others (2 Corinthians 11:25). Would the "faith teacher" of the contemporary world claim that Paul experienced suffering because he did not have faith enough to believe? If so, the claim would be preposterous. The apostle Paul and the other disciples were great men of faith.

However, they were often beaten and thrown into prison (Acts 3; Acts 12). Steven was a faith-filled follower of Christ, yet he was stoned to death (Acts 7:54-60). Job was a righteous man who respected God and was referred to as blameless (Job 1:1). Conversely, he battled fiery trials and suffered much loss. Thus, it is unbiblical to suggest that modern-day believers who suffer, like Paul and the others in the Bible who suffered, do so in all scenarios over a lack of faith.

Faith is crucial regarding a relationship with God and receiving divine intervention. Nevertheless, the faith factor fails to meet the biblical benchmark as the blame and source for *all* moments of suffering salvation. Cheap is the teaching that points the finger at every believer experiencing suffering, casting shame and guilt upon weak faith. Yet, the reason for suffering salvation is situational and weak faith can undoubtedly be a factor.

The heart of my journey into suffering salvation disclosed within this book is enveloped around the biblical concept that varying circumstances can contribute to suffering salvation due to differing details. There is no one-size-fits-all answer to suffering in the Bible. Can a lack of faith in various situations in the lives of believers contribute to suffering salvation? Yes. It is, therefore, expedient for the believer to develop and strengthen their faith by absorbing the Word of God on a regular basis (Romans 10:17). Likewise, it is fundamental for the believer to stand upon the promises of God (Hebrews 10:23), and to speak words of faith versus doubt and unbelief intentionally and recurrently (Romans 4:17).

However, are all circumstances of suffering salvation the result of a lack of faith? No. Are various instances of physical illness, traumatic suffering, or unsavory encounters permitted by God due to flabby faith and a lack of trust in God? Yes. In the meantime, it is deceptive and shallow to deem all matters of suffering salvation the direct result of a lack of faith. A holistic theological response to suffering salvation must incorporate numerous factors and possible circumstances. For this purpose, not every moment of suffering salvation can be pointed upon the weak faith believer.

However, to ignore the faith factor and inform hurting believers that faith does not matter is equally specious. Strong faith matters, and believers must develop faith by hearing the Word of God and then exercise their strong faith in a preventative fashion. A lack of strong faith can, in fact, contribute to periods of suffering salvation. Overall, the answer to why believers experience suffering salvation is as follows: It depends.

In the following chapter, our journey into understanding suffering salvation continues as we delve into life's trials and hardships.

Chapter 5
THE TRIALS OF LIFE

"Dear friends, do not be surprised at the fiery ordeal that has come on you to test you, as though something strange were happening to you. But rejoice inasmuch as you participate in the sufferings of Christ, so that you may be overjoyed when his glory is revealed" (1 Peter 4:12-13).

> According to the apostle Peter, believers should anticipate strenuous circumstances. This may run contrary to the western ideals of comfortable Christianity. However, Peter proclaims that difficult times should not shock the believer as being unordinary oddities.

Westernized biblical preaching often presents a picture of the middle-class good life. Common is the portrayal of existence with Christ materializing in the form of stylish clothes, padded bank accounts, comfortable vehicles, and the newest technological gadgets, along with painless living. Just imagine the generalized examples of sermon titles familiar in the contemporary context drawing interest, such as the blessing, how to cancel your debt, walking in joy, and living life happy and healthy.

While these are not specific titles directly sourced from quoted pastors, the widespread idea is discernable and recognizable to the modern-day western believer. In this western church environment, regrettably, believers are poised to gloss over scriptures that reveal the storm's value and the factual reality of the fiery trial.

Due to the relentless exposure to the happy life mentality within western church culture, the astonishment is profound when the believer encounters suffering salvation. Numerous believers stand stunned when facing the stark reality that roses do, in fact, have thorns. It is as if believers have been tutored to live the good life while rarely being prepared for the tumultuous side of the equation.

Most often, believers are frequently stunned by the reality of suffering salvation. I understand this firsthand. In the example of the loss of our first baby, we were most assuredly staggered by the shake-up of our storm because we had been taught to believe that faith-filled Christians do not experience agony.

Multiple moments I have sat with believers who have been traumatized by personal catastrophe. From midnight visits to the local fire department consoling weeping families crying around the dead body of the family member laying in a body bag, to the 2:00 am visits with families stunned by murdered loved ones. I have watched tears flow like rivers down the cheeks of the faithful, hearing the predictable gut-wrenching theological inquiry: Pastor, why would God allow this to happen? Each time this question is hurled toward my direction, the pain of the position is identifiable because I, too, have asked the provocative question in my moments of suffering salvation.

Does God desire the believer to be happy, healthy, and whole? Yes. The Bible is chalked full of scripture that indicates the affirmative. For instance, the apostle Paul informs that God desires His people to be abundantly blessed and equipped, "And God is able to bless you abundantly, so that in all things at all times, having all that you need, you will abound in every good work" (2 Corinthians 9:8).

The psalmist casts the generalization that God will bless the believer with heartfelt desires, "May he give you the desire of your heart and make all your plans succeed" (Psalm 20:4). Similarly, Luke reports that the people of God can be blessed to the overflow, "Give, and it will be given to you. A good measure, pressed down, shaken together, and running over, will be poured into your lap. For with the measure you use, it will be measured to you" (Luke 6:38).

The blessings of God are endless in supply for the believer, both physically and spiritually, "Praise be to the God and Father of our Lord Jesus Christ, who has blessed us in the heavenly realms with every spiritual blessing in Christ" (Ephesians 1:3). God desires believers to be blessed (Psalm 144:15), to walk in peace (Philippians 4:7), and to rejoice always (1 Thessalonians 5:16).

Equally, God desires believers to experience the joy of the Lord (Nehemiah 8:10), to be renewed with strength (Isaiah 40:31), and to live the abundant life (John 10:10). All of the aforesaid scriptural promises should be quoted, memorized, and claimed by faith within the life of the believer! This is a precise example of why the faith factor is important in believers' lives.

Simultaneously, the Bible is crammed full of scriptures that suggest balance, forewarning the believer that moments of suffering salvation will be commonplace, all while further instructing the attitude concerning suffering to be positive. Running parallel to scriptures concerning the good life are scriptures that warn the believer that fiery trials are a forgone conclusion (1 Peter 4:12-13). In reality, the concept of periodic Christian struggle revealed within the Bible slaps the mainstream mentality of western comfort Christianity boldly in the face. Trials and suffering are a portion of the believer's life.

Nevertheless, according to the Word, trials and suffering are both to be anticipated. This can be discovered as the apostle Paul instructs believers to rejoice in trials, "Not only so, but we also rejoice in our sufferings, because we know that suffering produces perseverance; perseverance, character; and character, hope" (Romans 5:3). The believer, in line with this passage, is to rejoice during trouble!

In addition to expecting suffering salvation, the apostle Paul elevates the matter by calling upon believers to rejoice in the midst of trials! *The attitude during the trial often determines the trajectory of the trial.* It is worthy of notation that the trouble experienced within life is not the object of rejoicing. In contrast, the purpose of rejoicing in the trial is the potential end results that the situation delivers for the believer's benefit.

God is not cruel. God never said to rejoice *because of* the suffering. God said to rejoice *over* the suffering. For instance, examine how the apostle Paul responds when he experiences suffering salvation,

> "I am more. I have worked much harder, been in prison more frequently, been flogged more

severely, and been exposed to death repeatedly. Five times I received from the Jews the forty lashes minus one. Three times I was beaten with rods, once I was pelted with stones, three times I was shipwrecked, I spent a night and a day in the open sea, I have been constantly on the move. I have been in danger from rivers, in danger from bandits, in danger from my fellow Jews, in danger from Gentiles; in danger in the city, in danger in the country, in danger at sea; and in danger from false believers. I have labored and toiled and have often gone without sleep; I have known hunger and thirst and have often gone without food; I have been cold and naked" (2 Corinthians 11:23-27).

This passage describes turmoil and suffering in the life of a Christian believer and leader.

However, Paul proceeds to reveal his response to suffering salvation after the discourse, "That is why, for Christ's sake, I delight in weaknesses, in insults, in hardships, in persecutions, in difficulties. For when I am weak, then I am strong" (2 Corinthians 12:10). This passage highlights a response of rejoicing *over* the suffering! Praise in the storm must be the mantra of the believer. There persists an attitude of praise during suffering salvation emerging from the life of Paul!

James makes a similar claim as he states,

> "Consider it pure joy, my brothers and sisters, whenever you face trials of many kinds, because

you know that the testing of your faith produces perseverance. Let perseverance finish its work so that you may be mature and complete, not lacking anything" (James 1:2-4).

Once again, the instruction from scripture is to rejoice in suffering, knowing that it serves to refine the believer.

Jesus further elevates the argument as He straightforwardly states that believers will, in fact, experience trouble, "I have told you these things, so that in me you may have peace. In this world you will have trouble. But take heart! I have overcome the world" (John 16:33). However, Jesus encourages those experiencing pain to rejoice!

Author and professor Derek Thomas speaks in affirmation of this aspect concerning suffering salvation as he shares,

> "It is not enough simply to acquiesce, to grin-and-bear the trials; we must learn to see suffering for what it accomplishes to the one who has faith. It is the perspective to which Paul turns in Romans 5: "we rejoice in our sufferings" (verse 3). And why *rejoice*? Because "suffering produces endurance, and endurance produces character, and character produces hope, and hope does not put us to shame, because God's love has been poured into our hearts through the Holy Spirit who has been given to us" (vv. 4-5). There is no hint of masochism in this statement, simply a resolve to view suffering as the vehicle through which God brings us to the purest form of our

existence – conformity to the image of Christ (Rom. 8:29) (Thomas, n.d., para. 44).

God teaches believers to rejoice in the pain, knowing that the pain produces character in Christ. Learn to rejoice in the suffering! There is potential power when the believer maintains a graceful attitude versus a hateful attitude in the face of pressure. This biblical teaching contrasts the idea of a faith-filled good life without trial.

Further, suffering is presented within scripture as having an empowering and refining effect. Fiery trials have a transformational repercussion on the believer. The Bible says that the trying of the faith produces patience (James 1:2-3). Notice that the Bible does not teach that the middle-class good life produces patience. Scripture affirms that there are some lessons in life that cannot be learned outside of the fiery trial. Likewise, some aspects of introspection and self-enhancement are the benefits of suffering salvation, which is seldom discovered in other forms. The trials of life enhance the believer. Period.

In various situations, suffering salvation builds the believer's resolve. However, the bar is raised within the storm to the level of rejoicing for the trouble! The rejoicing within the pain demonstrates growth and maturity in Christ. Perspective can alter the outcome of suffering salvation.

Additional underpinning to this aspect can be discovered as Peter claims that fiery trials are more precious to us than gold,

> "In all this you greatly rejoice, though now for a little while you may have had to suffer grief in all kinds of trials. Your faith-of greater worth than

gold, which perishes even though refined by fire—may result in praise, glory and honor when Jesus Christ is revealed" (1 Peter 1:6-7).

Peter continues as he states, "And the God of all grace, who called you to his eternal glory in Christ, after you have suffered a little while, will himself restore you and make you strong, firm and steadfast" (1 Peter 5:10). In a similar manner, James declares, "Blessed is the one who perseveres under trial because, having stood the test, that person will receive the crown of life that the Lord has promised to those who love him" (James 1:12).

Finally, Paul exhorts with an equal admonition, "Be joyful in hope, patient in affliction, faithful in prayer" (Romans 12:12). Thus, it can be extracted from the Word that suffering salvation, in assorted circumstances, attends to cultivate the believer. The pressure of the pain often produces a position of character in the believer.

Moving forward, the refiner's fire has been well documented. Books have been penned, songs have been coined, and aphorisms have been notoriously generated upon the matter. This book does not suggest that the refiner's fire is a new concept of study. However, the metaphor is drawn directly and decisively from scripture. For instance, the minor prophet states concerning God, "He will sit as a refiner and purifier of silver; he will purify the Levites and refine them like gold and silver. Then the Lord will have men who will bring offerings in righteousness" (Malachi 3:3).

The imagery is drawn from a refiner's fire, which the refiner melts down a metal, such as gold or silver, for purification purposes. Once a metal is in its melted-down state, the dross rises to the top and is removed from the metal before it cools (Palmer, 2020, para.

9-12). Thus, this is a process of refinement and purification. A refiner's fire does not destroy the metal; rather, it allows the junk within the metal to come up so that it can be removed. A refiner's fire does not consume the object. Instead, it enhances the metal and increases its value (Palmer, 2020, para. 9-12).

Several passages support the concept of casting God as being one who allows suffering, in diverse situations, to refine the believer, "See, I have refined you, though not as silver; I have tested you in the furnace of affliction" (Isaiah 48:10). Job cries out in his suffering with a similar voice, "But he knows the way that I take; when he has tested me, I will come forth as gold" (Job 23:10). Also, the psalmist sings in agreement, "For you, God, tested us; you refined us like silver" (Psalm 66:10). Heat brings forth impurities hidden within.

What comes to the surface during the heat of the refiner process exposes what is dormant. God often purifies His people in similar ways. God uses moments of suffering, sinfulness, and shortcomings to refine people in the imagery of a refiner's fire (Palmer, 2020, para. 9-12).

God permits periods of suffering salvation, in countless situations, to bring strength, transformation, introspection, and resolve to the believer. Most often, there is a lesson to be learned while the battle rages. Likewise, pressure and pain often bring forth patience and future potential. Through trials and challenging moments in life, believers build muscle and maturity. Believers must behold the message hidden in hardship. Suffering salvation is often a defining moment in multiple forms and fashions.

Conversely, the question remains: Why does God allow suffering trials and rich refiner's fire? A poignant answer is that some suffering is for the believer's ultimate benefit. Moreover, if God coddled and shielded all believers from each form of suffering, the church would be bursting with spineless and spoiled people. According to the Bible, God never inflicts pain or incites suffering.

However, God clearly contains the ability to intervene when His omniscience knows best. Remember, God knows the big picture. Therefore, if God chooses not to act on behalf of the believer, there could be a lesson in the fire. Look for the lesson and consider what might be learned. Simply stated some situations of suffering salvation result from life's trials.

The nucleus of my journey into suffering salvation disclosed within this book develops in the reoccurring theme of the biblical concept that varying circumstances can contribute to suffering salvation due to differing details. There is no one-size-fits-all answer to suffering in the Bible. In the same manner, a dominant question emerges within this chapter: Is every moment of suffering salvation the result of the trials of life? The answer is no. It is not biblically sound or theologically accurate to render all difficulties within life the result of the refiner. Poor preaching suggests that every period of pain stems from the refiner's fire or the permitted fiery trial.

Likewise, flawed counsel exhorts the hearer that God allowed their pain to teach a lesson in every circumstance. Equal is the argument that not all situations of suffering salvation include free will, the big picture, and the faith factor. Thus, not every example of suffering is the result of the trials of life. The one-size-fits-all form of counsel in the moments of suffering crisis needs to cease. A holistic theological response to suffering salvation must include multiple dimensions and possible circumstances. For that reason, not every moment of suffering salvation can be surmised as the trials of life.

Conversely, it is biblically accurate to admit that suffering salvation, in multiple different moments, is permitted by God as a result of the refiner's fire. It is biblically sound and theologically astute to infer the interpretation from scripture that some moments of suffering salvation are allowed by God to manifest, in order to refine, teach, transform, develop, or advance the maturity of the believer.

In other words, there are lessons to learn from the fire and maturity to be gained from the battle. The Bible fails to promise believers that following Christ equals a painless life. The popular preached image of a padded life complete with easy living is a form of false teaching. In contrast to the contemporary middle-class good life presented in a wide span of pulpits, serving Christ does include fiery trials and painful days.

Moreover, serving God does not mean a life excluded from pain. Receiving Jesus as savior never guarantees an easy life. Thus, some periods of suffering salvation can be understood in light of the trials of life. Actually, trials may heat up after following Jesus as spiritual warfare frequently increases and character often needs to be molded. Meanwhile, suffering salvation, in various moments, transpires due to God allowing believers to learn, grow, be challenged, mature, and transform from the pressure of the pain.

Does this idea equate to an evil angry God? No! God is love and free from flawed human emotions. God is not a divine loose cannon reacting out of spite and manipulation. However, in terms of suffering, it must be considered that free will, the big picture, and the faith factor all must be taken into theological understanding. Likewise, it must be regarded as being a possibility that God permits periods of pain in particular situations for the best interests of the believer in the form of development and fiery trials. Consequently, the battle's attitude frequently determines the outcome's altitude. Thus, learn to rejoice in the trials of life.

In the following chapter, our journey into understanding suffering salvation continues into the treacherous field of spiritual warfare.

Chapter 6
SPIRITUAL WARFARE

"For our struggle is not against flesh and blood, but against the rulers, against the authorities, against the powers of this dark world and against the spiritual forces of evil in the heavenly realms. Therefore, put on the full armor of God, so that when the day of evil comes, you may be able to stand your ground, and after you have done everything, to stand" (Ephesians 6:12-13).

> The apostle Paul directs this passage to the churches at Ephesus, warning believers of the stark reality concerning the spiritual entanglement against demonic forces. There is a fight that must waged and won through the victory that is available in Christ, or the damage will tangibly manifest.

Christians are in a war. Albeit an unseen war, Christians are in a spiritual entanglement, nonetheless. War is ugly.

War can be deadly. War can be life-altering. Moreover, war must be taken seriously. The person who scoffs at war is one who is devastated by its potential.

Similar to the concept of literal war, spiritual warfare can be perilous. As he writes to the believers at Ephesus, the process of recognizing the impact of Paul's warning begins with the realization that forces of evil in the spiritual realm are actively advancing against God's people. Thus, spiritual warfare is an actuality within the lives of believers. Period. This is a foremost fact that must not be disregarded in the journey of understanding suffering salvation.

Human beings have an enemy. This is the truth concerning the behind-the-scenes of human life. Satan is real. Jesus discloses the intensity of the satanic agenda against God's people as He states, "The thief comes only to steal and kill and destroy" (John 10:10). Fallen angels are real (Jude 1:6; 2 Peter 2:4). Demons are real (1 Timothy 4:1; Acts 16:16-19; James 2:19; Matthew 8:31; Luke 8:30). These spiritual realities are not folklore or sci-fi fantasy. The demonic are positioned in hatred toward humanity, maintaining the destructive desire to steal and ruin. Any believer who denies this aspect of spiritual certainty is putting their proverbial head in the sand and accepting defeat.

Furthermore, spiritual warfare is more authentic than the physically discernable, while the war remains unseen. Spiritual warfare is to be received as a somber warning and a call to arms. Warfare in the spirit is a reality; therefore, it needs to be recognized as solemn and significant. Making this point transparent, Paul teaches that believers wrestle against rulers, authorities, powers of this dark world, and against the spiritual forces of evil in the heavenly realms (Ephesians 6:12).

Meanwhile, Paul portrays this prolific battle in wrestling imagery (Ephesians 6:12). Furthermore, this is the only passage in the New Testament where this specific Greek word for wrestling is penned (Strong's, 1890, G3823). The original audience of Paul's letter within the Ephesus church context would have captured the solemn warning hidden within the passage more rapidly than the contemporary reader because, in that particular culture, wrestling was a gruesome and potentially deadly ancient combat sports event within the Isthmian games (Arvanitis, 2003). Moreover, this form of wrestling was hand-to-hand combat, not a contemporary version of holds, maneuvers, and strength displays (Arvanitis, 2003).

Elevating the intensity of this ancient version of wrestling, the loser of the Isthmian match would often have their eyes gouged out. In other words, Paul is applying this analogy to enlighten the believer that spiritual warfare is intense, authentic, and profound. The enemy desires to win and destroy humanity! While Paul is not suggesting that believers literally wrestle with demons as did the ancient Isthmian competitors with physical opponents, he is disclosing through imagery the momentousness of the issue at hand.

Furthering the argument, the apostle Peter waves the warning concerning the gravity of spiritual warfare as he declares, "Be alert and of sober mind. Your enemy the devil prowls around like a roaring lion looking for someone to devour" (1 Peter 5:8). The enemy desires to destroy the lives of believers. According to Peter, Satan is ever searching for an opportunity to bring calamity into the lives of those who trust in Jesus. The entirety of the context concerning the noted passages offers both the reality and the seriousness of spiritual warfare.

Conversely, understanding the potential impacts of spiritual warfare upon instances of suffering salvation requires an unpacking of spiritual warfare in its biblical essence. Thus, good teaching on the authenticity of spiritual warfare does not mandate an excessive elevation of over-emphasis upon demonology. Believers must resign from the ideology that there is a devil in every doorknob and a demon behind all demonstrations.

Satan is not omnipresent. Therefore, Satan is not simultaneously attacking every believer daily. The well-rehearsed rhetorical line that the devil is fighting me today is inaccurate. Satan cannot attack each believer every day because Satan is not everywhere all the time. In the same vein, demons are not the sole source of each diagnosis of sickness, and demons are not the instigators of every flat tire. In the same way, demons are not the contributor to every difficult day experienced, and demons are not the cause of all cancerous deaths. Such an over-emphasis upon all things demon and devil does not represent sound theology.

In a theological sense, demonology is defined as the study of demons (McKim, 1996, p. 73). In a practical application, demonology is an unhealthy fixation on blaming all negative experiences upon demons, coupled with an overemphasis upon all things Satan. While spiritual warfare is real, this book does not promote an unhealthy preoccupation with demonology. Further, an excellent example of unfortunate spiritual warfare teaching would be to blame *all* instances of suffering salvation upon demons or Satan.

In other words, not all suffering salvation results from spiritual warfare. Are various instances of cancer demonically driven, thus resulting in suffering salvation? Yes. Does the Bible support the reality of instances in which suffering in the lives of believers originates from demonic warfare? Yes.

However, are all instances of suffering salvation the result of demonic activity? No. Demons are a reality. Satan hates human beings. Conversely, avoiding an over-emphasis on demonology and hyper spirituality is necessary to remain within the realm of solid biblical belief.

Equally important, good teaching on the authenticity of spiritual warfare must include that spiritual warfare is not a war against people. Contemporary Christianity must move beyond viewing spouses, friends, neighbors, fellow church members, opposing denominations, foreign national powers, national powers, state powers, and municipal powers as being *the* enemy.

On the same side of the coin, the church must move past regarding democrats, republicans, independents, unbelievers, atheists, doubters, scoffers, homosexuals, or any other various examples of people or groups as being *the* enemy. Spiritual warfare is not a war against people. Rather, it is against principalities, powers, against the rulers of the darkness of this world, and against spiritual wickedness in high places (Ephesians 6:12-13).

The fight that Christians wage is not against flesh and blood. Paul adds transparency to this argument as he states, "The weapons we fight with are not the weapons of the world. On the contrary, they have divine power to demolish strongholds" (2 Corinthians 10:4). Quarrels and fights with other people are understood as moments of interpersonal conflict (James 4:1), which is another topic for a different book. However, believers must underscore the actuality that spiritual warfare is not waged against people.

Going further, to offer a concise exegetical unpacking of Ephesians 6:12-13 granting a solid understanding of the topic, it must be recognized that Paul is disclosing four levels of demonic warfare in a de-escalating pattern within the passage. The powers that believers war against are listed in this context in descending order, offering a vague listing of the ranks within the demonic armies (Bible Study Tools, n.d.).

In an effort to examine the four ranks of demons disclosed by Paul, the first listed in the passage is principalities. This word in the Greek means a commencement: chief, concrete, beginning, the first (Strong's, 1890, G746). This word choice appears to indicate a top level of evil spiritual forces. Thus, the word can be understood as the beginning, the origin, the person or thing that commences, the first person or thing in a series, or the leader.

In other words, this is the chief power in the spiritual realm. The average Christian who is not praying, studying, fasting, inviting, witnessing, working for God, or helping to advance the kingdom in any form is not likely to ever "wrestle" with this category of demons. Casual Christians do not "wrestle" with principalities. The indication would be that this level of spiritual attack would be reserved for those positively impacting the kingdom of darkness in a spiritually aggressive form.

Second, Paul continues the de-escalating pattern as he employs the word powers (Ephesians 6:12-13). In the Greek, this word means delegated influence: authority, jurisdiction, liberty, power (Strong's, 1890, G1849). The word powers employed in this context refers to general forces of evil attacking believers in the form of taking power away, such as through bondage or addiction. These demons within spiritual warfare take power over people, as people yield their members (bodies) to sin and addiction (Romans 6:13).

This highlights why Paul emphasizes the importance of believers to avoid bondage and choose to walk in freedom, "Stand fast therefore in the liberty by which Christ has made us free, and do not be entangled again with a yoke of bondage" (Galatians 5:1 NKJV). Believers must accept the reality that some instances of suffering salvation are the direct result of bondage and addiction. God is not at fault for these situations and examples of suffering.

Third, Paul furthers the de-escalating pattern as he employs the word rulers (Ephesians 6:12-13). In the Greek, this word means a world ruler: an epithet of Satan (Strong's, 1890, G2888). This word choice indicates that a world ruler is a demon who has authority over regions, nations, states, cities, villages, areas, or perhaps even neighborhoods. Specifically, this would be the category of demons that bring oppression to a particular area.

Perhaps you have read testimonies of missionaries discerning various regional demons holding oppression over different nations while doing missionary work. In the same manner, Paul makes this known so that believers can discern various attacks and forms of spiritual oppression. Demons are real, and they most assuredly can have a negative impact on people and regions.

Forth, Paul concludes the de-escalating categorization of demons as he speaks of spiritual wickedness in high places (Ephesians 6:12-13). The Greek word choice for this category of demons indicates moral depravity (Strong's, 1890, G4189). This form of spiritual attack can be identified as low-level demons who tempt people with depravity: wickedness, evil, sins, and iniquity. Hence, these are demons who lead people into moral depravity by deceit (Matthew 26:41; Hebrews 4:15), tricks (Matthew 4:1-11), and sinful temptations (Ephesians 6:16). Demons work to tempt people into sin and into making imprudent decisions.

Meanwhile, prayerless people do not win spiritual fights. Believers who fail to read the Word do not win spiritual fights. Believers who fail to guard their minds and align their thoughts and words with the truth of the Bible do not win spiritual battles (2 Corinthians 10:5; Romans 12:1-2). Spiritually lazy people are defeated, people.

Moving forward, an authentic discussion about the understanding of spiritual warfare in terms of how it applies to suffering salvation must simultaneously include a concise review of angles. While refusing to delve into an over-emphasis upon angelology, it must not be overlooked, in the discussion of spiritual warfare, that angelic beings fight in the unseen realm against demonic beings on behalf of believers (Psalm 91:11; Psalm 34:7; Hebrews 1:14; Luke 22:43).

Angelology is defined as a study of the doctrine of angels (McKim, 1996, p. 11). Sound theology does not shy away from a balanced view of the existence and activity of angels. However, an overemphasis on angels can give way to the extreme end of the spectrum. This book does not advance an overemphasis on angels in discussing suffering salvation. Conversely, according to scripture, it must be considered that angels do war in the spirit on behalf of the hurting believer.

Further, in some instances where it appears that God might be ignoring a believer who is caught in a moment of suffering, one must recognize that things in the natural do not always appear as they are in the supernatural. For instance, Daniel prayed and sacrificed for 21 days waiting to hear from God, who could arguably appear to be distant and aloof. Yet, the angel appeared unto Daniel with a counter message,

> "Do not be afraid, Daniel. Since the first day that you set your mind to gain understanding and to humble yourself before your God, your words

> were heard, and I have come in response to them. But the prince of the Persian kingdom resisted me twenty-one days. Then Michael, one of the chief princes, came to help me, because I was detained there with the king of Persia. Now I have come to explain to you what will happen to your people in the future, for the vision concerns a time yet to come" (Daniel 10:10-14).

This passage indicates that a fight in the spirit realm hindered the answer to prayer. The possibilities of angelic assistance and warfare in the spirit must be considered when entangled with suffering salvation.

On the other hand, an authentic discussion of spiritual warfare as it pertains to periods of suffering salvation must go one step further and transparently denounce the idea that God is caught up in a cosmic fight. God is not locked into a galactic battle. It is cartoonish and mythical to fathom God tugging back and forth with Satan and demons. Period. God is matchless. God is mighty and inconceivable. God reigns as the one true ineffable, creating, and sovereign God.

Truthfully, a demon is no match for God. Demons tremble before our God (James 2:19). Demons obey the command of our God (Matthew 8:28-34). God is perfect, holy, complete, omniscient, and omnipotent. In fact, Satan and demons are trivial compared to the timeless and matchless God of all creation. Demons bow to our God, and Satan flees from our God.

Moreover, Jesus is presented within scripture as possessing all power and all authority in heaven and on Earth (Matthew 28:18). Bolstering the argument; Paul gives powerful points concerning God in the matter of spiritual warfare as he declares,

"And you, being dead in your trespasses and the uncircumcision of your flesh, He has made alive together with Him, having forgiven you all trespasses, having wiped out the handwriting of requirements that was against us, which was contrary to us. And He has taken it out of the way, having nailed it to the cross. Having disarmed principalities and powers, He made a public spectacle of them, triumphing over them in it" (Colossians 2:13-15 NKJV).

Note the phraseology within this passage concerning the defeat of the enemy: disarmed, public spectacle, and triumphing over. The word disarmed, as it is defined in the Greek, means despoiled: ruined, took away its power (Strong's, 1890, G554). Public spectacle, described in Greek, means making a show of, exhibiting, or embarrassing (Strong's, 1890, G1165).

Even so, the phrase triumphing over as it is defined in the Greek, means to make an acclamatory procession: to conquer, to parade the victory of conquering (Strong's, 1890, G2358). Do any of these words or phrases indicate a God struggling in warfare with Satan and demons? No! God has defeated the enemy! Frankly, it never was a fight, to begin with. In the fullness of time, God acted, and it was over! The truth concerning spiritual warfare involves knowing that God is not fighting in spiritual warfare! God is victorious. Period. God is almighty, and there is no match to Him.

Spiritual warfare, then, is defined and understood as being an ongoing battle between believers and demons. It is an unseen war that is waged between believers and the enemy (Ephesians

6:12). Spiritual warfare is not a spiritual fight between God and Satan. Instead, it is a spiritual battle between people and demons led and fueled by Satan (1 Peter 5:8; John 10:10). Believers may experience suffering salvation, in assorted situations, due to the loss of spiritual warfare stemming from lazy Christianity, a lack of a regular lifestyle of prayer, and a deficit of submitting to God and rebuking the enemy (James 4:7).

God always makes a way of escape for the believer in each temptation and promises that no temptation would be permitted so intense that rejection is not possible (1 Corinthians 10:13). However, this does not guarantee that all believers will fight the good fight, rebuke the enemy (James 4:7), cast down imaginations (2 Corinthians 10:5), and plug into the Word of God on a regular basis (Romans 10:17). Thus, some forms of suffering salvation occur at the cause of spiritual warfare.

However, the question of practicality remains within the discussion of spiritual warfare in terms of prevention and waging war in the vein of suffering salvation; how do believers fight in spiritual warfare? Imagine the defeat of any military engaged in combat if the soldiers failed to recognize the presence of the enemy or correctly utilized the weapons of warfare. Furthermore, imagine the confusion, calamity, and chaos that would ensue if the army was not adequately trained on the weapons within the engagement arsenal. The response to the rhetorical imagination is obvious. The military would experience defeat, overwhelming defeat.

This analogy applies equally as this is frequently the case with believers and spiritual warfare. It is common for believers to fail in knowing how to engage in spiritual warfare, resulting in defeat, which can often manifest as suffering salvation. Believers

Suffering Salvation

resemble a useless, defeated, chaotic military when the enemy is not recognized, the weapons of warfare are not engaged, and spiritual victory is squandered by lazy application of biblical responsibilities.

So then, how is spiritual warfare successfully engaged in a practical means as it pertains to suffering salvation? First, Paul says in Ephesians 6:10 to stand strong in the lord. Spiritual warfare is not won by engaging in a lethargic tactic. Spiritual victories are won, in contrast, when believers rely upon God (Ephesians 6:10), stay close in prayer (Psalm 91:1-2), rebuke the enemy (James 4:7), and walk in authority granted to each believer in Jesus (Mark 16:16-18). Failing to apply these principles is equal to a willful acceptance of defeat.

Can God be blamed for moments of suffering salvation that is the result of a believer's ignorance in the knowledge of fighting spiritual warfare? Is every moment of suffering salvation the result of this willful defeat and self-sabotage? No. Are some moments of suffering salvation the result of an insufficiency of application concerning these spiritual warfare principles? Yes.

All believers can be assured of the following encouraging biblical facts: You are not helpless in your battle! You are not defenseless in your battle! You are not alone in your battle! However, simply stating a belief in God and faithfully attending church fails to apply the tools necessary to win the fight! Believers must actively take authority over demons and verbally rebuke them (Matthew 8:28-34; Acts 16:16-18; Mark 16:17). Believers must actively read the Bible and apply the tools granted (Romans 10:17). Believers must actively maintain closeness with God and choose to dwell in the secret place (Psalm 91:1-2). In other words, action must be engaged in terms of spiritual warfare, or defeat might be the manifestation.

Second, Paul teaches believers in the letter of 2 Corinthians that much spiritual warfare occurs in the mind. Stating that much spiritual warfare takes place in the mind is not equivalent to suggesting that spiritual warfare is mythical or psychological hogwash. Rather, Paul is disclosing the issue of casting down thoughts and refusing to accept each destructive, deceptive, manipulative, or condemning thought stemming from the source of personal belief. Examine what the apostle states concerning this critical aspect of spiritual warfare,

> "For the weapons of our warfare are not carnal but mighty in God for pulling down strongholds, casting down arguments and every high thing that exalts itself against the knowledge of God, bringing every thought into captivity to the obedience of Christ" (2 Corinthians 10:4-6 NKJV).

This passage contains clear textual evidence that demons fight believers in the thought life. Demons lie, condemn, contort, blame, cast doubt, cast seeds of jealousy, manipulate, and tempt in the mind of those who know Christ as savior. Nonetheless, personal responsibility remains to cast negative and demonic thoughts down and fight the good fight of faith.

Notice that the apostle states in the passage above that the weapons of warfare are not physical but spiritual. The enemy lies, gives false thoughts, manipulates, and attempts to sway away from the truth in the mind. People are driven to think defeated thoughts, believe lies, make poor decisions, get into anger, lash out in frustration, and make self-destructive choices that work to manipulate their emotions.

Believers are tempted into disobedience and sin by warfare in the mind. Much spiritual warfare is a mental battle of dealing with what demons bring to the mind. Not all temptation into sin indeed emerges from demonic thoughts in the mind, as the Bible teaches that desire for sin also stems from the heart and one's internal desires (James 1:13-15; Matthew 15:18-20).

However, the demonic spiritual war for the mind is nonetheless noteworthy. Remember, the thought life contributes to speaking words and taking actions. Thus, if believers do not deal with the thought planted in the mind by demons, eventually, correlating words will be spoken and actions will be taken. In so much, speaking negative words stemming from negative thoughts in the mind can afford situations in life to the enemy's plan (Proverbs 18:21; Romans 4:17). Accordingly, it is important to understand that words and confessions matter greatly within the discussion of spiritual warfare!

How do believers defeat the warfare in the mind? How do believers win this fight? How do believers get victory? The answer is taking thoughts captive and speaking the authority of the Word of God! When Paul instructs believers to take every thought into captivity (2 Corinthians 10:5), the word penned in the Greek means to make captive: to lead away captive (Strong's, 1890, G163). Therefore, the idea portrayed in fighting spiritual warfare is to take the thought over, get rid of it, or remove it. Yes, this requires work and discipline on behalf of the believer.

However, cannot the legitimate argument be established that many lazy or unlearned believers follow negative thoughts, speak negative words in correlation, and engage in ensuing negative actions, all of which can, at times, lead to manifestations of suffering salvation? If this is the case in various moments of suffering salvation, God cannot be made culpable for the agony.

Going further, winning the spiritual battle in the mind is accomplished by taking the thought captive and by the imperative effort of replacing the thought with the truth. The believer must maintain the thought life in correlation with the words of life instructed by Paul in his epistle to the Philippians as he implores, "Finally, brothers and sisters, whatever is true, whatever is noble, whatever is right, whatever is pure, whatever is lovely, whatever is admirable—if anything is excellent or praiseworthy—think about such things" (Philippians 4:8). Spiritual warfare is won by a strict allowance of maintaining only positive, constructive thoughts within the mind.

The biblical aspect of directing thoughts and renewing the mind in Christ has extra-biblical support in the realm of psychological teaching and literature. For instance, psychology supports the process of metacognition. By definition, metacognition refers to the methods used to plan, monitor, and assess one's understanding and performance. Metacognition includes a critical awareness of one's thinking and learning how to direct and improve one's thinking (Chick, n.d., para. 1-2). This psychological principle applies to the biblical application as believers intentionally cast down thoughts and learn to think like God, causing the brain to change. Casting affirmation to the idea of directing thoughts, author William Yount states,

> "Focusing our attention 'in Christ Jesus' on the actions, values, and principles of Scripture creates, for lack of a better term, a more biblical brain, which 'naturally' supports a biblical lifestyle. With the application of mental force, the brain takes over repetitive thoughts, requiring less mental

effort to think them. We might well consider such a process the neurological aspect of sanctification. But God does not only speak to us through Scripture. He speaks to us directly through the medium of dreams and conscious thoughts. As His mind speaks to ours, and we attend to what He says, our brains weave the circuits to think His thoughts" (Yount, 2010, p. 538).

Accordingly, the process of renewing the mind supported within scripture and the spiritual warfare principles of casting down demonic thoughts while maintaining a positive mental stance finds merit in psychological teaching supporting mind renewal and thought directives. Renewing the mind, maintaining positive thoughts (Philippians 4:8), directing words, and changing correlating behavior are strong points in healthy spiritual warfare.

In my experience serving as a lead pastor during moments of counseling, it has been commonplace for the recipient to retort this line of counsel with the anecdotal reply, "It is easier said than done." Indeed, winning spiritual warfare is not easy as it calls for intentional action. It does require a deliberate effort.

However, the burdensome work of casting down demonically planted thoughts (2 Corinthians 10:5-6), dwelling on the truth of scripture (Philippians 4:8), speaking words of life (Romans 4:17), rebuking the enemy (James 4:7), and living life spiritually on guard (1 Peter 5:8) unquestionably outweighs living in dreadful defeat. Likewise, it overshadows experiencing suffering salvation at the hand of poor words and damaging decisions. As the old adage states: Anything worthwhile requires effort.

The essence of my journey into understanding suffering

salvation disclosed within this book incessantly tackles the biblical concept that varying circumstances can contribute to suffering salvation due to differing details. There is no one-size-fits-all answer to suffering in the Bible. Likewise, the subsequent question remains in direct response to our discussion concerning spiritual warfare: Is every moment of suffering salvation the result of demonic activity and the loss of the battle of the mind? The answer is no. The devil is not to blame in every account of suffering salvation.

Are selected accounts of suffering salvation the direct result of demons? Yes. Are various instances of physical illness and suffering brought on by demons or Satan? Yes. Can it be said that diverse occurrences of tragedies befall as the result of the enemy? Yes. Is it biblical to suggest that the devil is behind specific battles in the life of the believer? Yes. Is it true that some people are demon-possessed, leading to horrific outcomes standing in need of deliverance? Absolutely.

However, can we lay the blame for all moments concerning suffering salvation at the feet of demons? No. Blaming every single occurrence that is negative, traumatic, and unfortunate on the devil is pitiful theology. Simultaneously, do considerable amounts of believers suffer as the result of the self-induced failure to cast down thoughts and overcome the mental battle? Yes.

Conversely, not every instance of suffering salvation is the result of spiritual warfare. Every experience of suffering salvation cannot be concluded as the result of free will, the big picture, the faith factor, or the refiner's fire. Likewise, all encounters of suffering salvation do not result from spiritual warfare. The one-size-fits-all form of counsel in the moments suffering salvation must cease. A holistic theological response to suffering must include multiple dimensions and possible circumstances.

For that reason, not every moment of suffering salvation can be surmised as the result of spiritual warfare. Yet, it must be concluded that various examples of suffering salvation do transpire because of failed encounters of spiritual warfare in the lives of believers. Consequently, believers must make the intentional decision to stand and fight the good fight of faith (Ephesians 6:13)!

Believers should carry the mentality that demons will not win today by choosing to intentionally advance the authority that resides within through Christ Jesus (Matthew 8:28-34; Acts 16:16-18; Mark 16:17). Stand up and take arms in the spirit. Cast off lazy living in Christ and win the battle waging within the thought life by casting down thoughts and speaking authority (Philippians 4:8; 2 Corinthians 10: 5-6).

Our journey into embracing an understanding of suffering salvation continues in the following chapter, as we tackle arguably the most uncomfortable and disregarded topic in the world of Christian suffering: chastisement.

Chapter 7
A TALK WITH DAD

"Because the LORD disciplines the one He loves, and He chastens everyone He accepts as His son. Endure hardship as discipline; God is treating you as His children" (Hebrews 12:6-8).

> The anonymous author of Hebrews, written to people who knew scripture extremely well (Johnson, 2010, p. 407), indicates that God, as father, will discipline His children. True love will correct. True love will guide. True love will warn. God, if anything, is the perfect model of a true loving father who refuses to withhold the guide of loving discipline.

Chastisement is an uncomfortable guest at the table of convenient Christian discussion. In the contemporary world of felt needs Christianity, chastisement is not a popular subject. Accordingly, people do not often hear sermons on the topic of chastisement. The following statement is merely anecdotal; however, prominent healthy churches with growing crowds seldom advertise an upcoming sermon series upon the joys of chastisement! One could argue that the palpable excitement of such a sermon series might be as popular as fried liver recipes or beet juice cleansing tips! In other words, chastisement is an unpopular and often overlooked aspect of theology. As a result, chastisement is, arguably, one of the least understood teachings within scripture. Thus, chastisement has been held in reserve for the final lens of our exploration into understanding suffering salvation.

What does the writer of Hebrews mean by the word chastisement? What is biblically balanced teaching upon this uneasy topic? Does God punish believers for their sins by sending periods of suffering salvation? These are all legitimate questions that deserve evaluation in discussing suffering salvation.

Have you ever heard a fellow church member suggest that someone across the pew has experienced suffering salvation due to sin and personal failure? In reference to the death of our baby, my wife was informed by an incorrect Christian that the death was provoked by sin on her part. Prodding even deeper, have you ever deliberated inwardly during the private moments of the night wondering if your period of pain befell at the hand of God's punishment for sin?

Driving to the heart of the subject, chastisement is not a rage of anger from God. Chastisement is not a moment in which God lashes out at His people with a divine rod of iron. Moreover, God does not punish believers. *Receive this truth!* God is not a human (John 4:24; Numbers 23:19). Therefore, absent from the nature of God are outbursts of emotional anger, rage, manipulation, punishment, or any other flawed expressive human expression.

God is not sitting distantly upon the throne of the heavens overlooking humanity, merely waiting for a moment to crush due to sins and failure. The one true living God is not vindictive and harsh in the manner of a cruel King on Earth.

Furthermore, chastisement is not punishment. Allow this argument to be made unequivocally. God does not punish believers for their sins. Suggesting that believers experience suffering salvation at the hand of a punishing God is a misappropriation of scripture and a form of psychologically damaging theology. God is not brutal, unjust, or malicious. God is not angry. Away with the characterization of God pacing back and forth in the throne room of heaven, fuming with vindictive anger over the sins of His people. The suggested images of an incensed, aloof, and punishing God must be removed from this discussion.

As a matter of fact, the Bible says that Jesus took the suffering and the punishment for the believer's sins upon the cross! This is foundational within scripture as the prophet declares, "But He *was* wounded for our transgressions, *He was* bruised for our iniquities; The chastisement for our peace *was* upon Him, And by His stripes, we are healed" (Isaiah 53:5 NKJV). *Read that scripture again!* The punishment for sin was *settled* upon the cross!

Likewise, the apostle Paul elevates the good news of the gospel, declaring with further affirmation that the punishment of believers was placed upon Jesus in a past tense format as he states,

> "When you were dead in your sins and in the uncircumcision of your flesh, God made you alive with Christ. He forgave us all our sins, having canceled the charge of our legal indebtedness, which stood against us and condemned us; he has

taken it away, nailing it to the cross" (Colossians 2:13-14).

Paul decrees that sin has been settled upon the cross! This is the good news of the gospel. Remove the image of God as being incensed and enraged in a penalizing fashion.

Moreover, the apostle Peter grants continued agreement upon the matter as he states that Christ suffered for the punishment of sin, "For Christ also suffered once for sins, the righteous for the unrighteous, to bring you to God. He was put to death in the body but made alive in the Spirit" (1 Peter 3:18). Jesus suffered once for sins upon the cross. The punishment for our sins was placed upon Him. Anyone who decides to receive the free gift of salvation by faith in Christ has been unchained from the penalty of their sins (Ephesians 2:8-9: Romans 10:9-10; John 3:16-17).

The late C. H. Spurgeon supports the argument that God never punishes believers for their sins as he states,

> "God's people can never by any possibility be punished for their sins. God has punished them already in the person of Christ, their substitute, has endured the full penalty for all their guilt, and neither the justice nor the love of God can ever exact again that which Christ has paid. Punishment can never happen to a child of God in the judicial sense, he can never be brought before God as his Judge, as charged with guilt, because that guilt was long ago transferred to the shoulders of Christ, and the punishment was exacted at the hands of his surety" (Spurgeon, 1855, para. 1).

Suffering Salvation

The words from Spurgeon are valid and supported by scripture. Therefore, God never sends moments of suffering salvation to believers as a form of punishment for their sins. Bury the burden and break the bonds of the self-inflicted pain of believing God is punishing you by directing suffering salvation upon your life.

Even so, the vehicle collision, the dead baby, and the loved one dying of cancer all fail to be legitimate biblical examples of God slapping His people with punishment. Likewise, the instance of rape, the house fire, the moment of spousal abuse, the murdered son, the overdose death, the cruel and inhuman moment of human trafficking, and the case of lung disease all fail to be legitimate biblical examples of God striking people with periods of suffering salvation as the result of punishment for sin!

However, a forthright consideration concerning the topic of chastisement as it is concerned with suffering salvation must grapple with the Old Testament complexities, which appear to contradict the stance that a good God does not punish believers for their sins. This journey into understanding suffering salvation will not cower away from the complex portions of the discussion.

For instance, 2 Samuel 12:15 states that God struck Bathsheba's baby, and he died due to the secret sin of David. The word came to David that his hidden sins of adultery and murder had been forgiven, but that open punishment for his sins would manifest in the form of God striking the baby, causing death (2 Samuel 12:12-23). This passage, quite frankly, appears to position God as guilty of the cruel and inhuman murder of an innocent baby.

How does this passage reconcile with a good God who does not punish believers for their sins? Offering a concise exegetical unpacking of this topic, the Hebrew word for "struck" in 2 Samuel 12:15 means to smite or inflict (Strong's, 1890, H5062). It implies causing sickness to come upon. Furthermore, this is the Hebrew word utilized in Exodus when God caused plagues to come upon Egypt when Pharoah refused to let God's people go in freedom (Exodus 11:4-5). Thus, the Hebrew word of choice by the author appears to be literal in the representation that God stuck or killed David's baby.

Accordingly, several traditional interpretations of this passage appear to allude to the idea that God struck the baby, sparing the life of ensuing ridicule and embarrassment being David's illegitimate adulterous child by granting immediate access to heaven (Geisler and Howe, 1992, para. 2). However, this interpretation, while serving to be mildly comfortable and convenient, lacks biblical and even moral consistency. Beyond suitability and idealism in the interpretation, this traditional extraction portrays God as a baby murderer!

Accordingly, the common conclusion presented cannot be correct, and the corresponding scriptures provide strong argumentation for biblical accuracy. In fact, Ezekiel 18:20 declares that the soul that sins shall die, and the son shall not share the guilt of the father. This being the case, the prophet Ezekiel disagrees with the common interpretation of God killing David's baby due to the issue of David's sin. According to Ezekiel, the sins of David would not move God to kill his baby as a form of punishment. Indeed, Jesus makes it further transparent that a person's trouble is not directly the result of the parent's sins (John 9:3). Hence, it cannot be biblically concluded that God killed David's baby as a form of chastisement. God does not kill people as a form of suffering salvation!

Instead, a proper reading, study, meditation, and prayer process will reveal a more insightful and consistent interpretation of this Old Testament dilemma found in 2 Samuel chapter 12, as it is concerned with an understanding of chastisement and suffering salvation. For instance, the context of the time reveals that the author of the passage elaborates on the mindset of King David and those who lived at that period in Earth's history. At that time in history, it was common for people to attribute to God what God allowed but did not directly cause (Armstrong, 2019).

On the same side of the coin, people in this ancient day considered God's passive allowance equal to God's active actions. In other words, an event of death that transpired in that period would be considered an act of God because God did not stop the death. An example of this interpretation would be the death of King Saul, who was king before David. King Saul committed suicide, and the Bible faithfully records this act (1 Samuel 31:4).

However, the Bible simultaneously describes King Saul's death in a different passage as God killing him (1 Chronicles 10:13-14). God did not kill King Saul. On the contrary, King Saul took his own life (1 Samuel 31:4). Yet, the author of 1 Chronicles, speaking through the thinking of that time period, records the event as though God forced King Saul to commit suicide.

In a similar notion, the narrative concerning the death of David's baby does not state how the infant would die, only that the infant was struck by God despite David's prayers. Consider a differing perspective of this passage. The pronouncement from the prophet that the child would die was an announcement of what God foreknew would transpire. It was a prediction of future events. Accordingly, it was not a judicial finding with the subsequent execution of the baby by God (Armstrong, 2019). In the greater context, 2 Samuel chapter 12 does not indicate that God would kill the child or cause the child's death, but rather that

God knew the child would die and that God would refrain from miraculous intervention to save the child (Armstrong, 2019). God did not kill the baby; He allowed the baby to die without His help.

In further discussion of the grappling with chastisement in the Old Testament as it applies to the understanding of suffering salvation, it also must be recalled that in the Old Testament, God dealt directly with sin, absent of a mediator between humankind and sin. Even so, chastisement is not to be understood as God punishing people in a direct active fashion. Believers can rest assured: God will not murder as a form of suffering salvation!

However, it can be interpreted from Old Testament scripture that God may passively allow an unfortunate situation to transpire without His intervention resulting in the manifestation of suffering salvation. *God choosing to permit action is not equal to God sending an action.*

Furthering the same lines of consideration on the image of mediation, it must be understood that God dealt with the depravity of sin directly in the Old Testament. Conversely, in the New Testament, there stands a mediator between the holiness of God and the depravity of sin in the person of Jesus Christ (1 Timothy 2:5). This mediation serves as a place of punishment. Jesus took the punishment for humanity of sin upon Himself. This is the rationale for the argument that chastisement is not punishment for sin.

In the same vein, the apostle Paul exclaims that Jesus did in the flesh what all of humanity was too weak to accomplish in the flesh. Jesus fulfilled the judicial law of God resulting in pardon and grace for sin when people freely receive by faith,

> "For what the law could not do I that it was weak through the flesh, God did by sending

His own Son in the likeness of sinful flesh, on account of sin: He condemned sin in the flesh that the righteous requirement of the law might be fulfilled in us who walk according to the flesh but according to the Spirit" (Romans 8:3-4).

Thus, scripture affirms that chastisement is not equal to God punishing believers for their sins. Accordingly, the argument is secure that God did not send suffering salvation into your life due to sins and failures.

What about Acts chapter 5 when God seemingly killed Ananias and Sapphira (Acts 5:1-11)? This is a strange passage where it appears that God strikes this man and his wife in death because they lied to God in the presence of Peter the apostle. Truthfully, this odd passage absent of opportunity for grace, confession, and forgiveness presents cause for the raising of the eyebrow. The passage stands in contrast to the attitude of Jesus in John when the women is caught in adultery (John 8:1-11). Where is the grace presented by Jesus of not casting stones? It must be considered that the oddity of this passage truly makes the narrative non-normative. Meaning, God does not continue this as a normal pattern in the lives of people. Proving the point, this scene is not repeated in the New Testament as normal. In other words, this type of response is not found again in the Bible.

Further, the shock and fear of the witnesses underscores the oddity and non-normative nature of the event (Acts 5: 5;11). Thus, something more must be at play. A complete exegetical extraction of this passage is not in the purview of suffering salvation.

However, what must be considered is the context of chapter 5. The chapter is filled with great levels of awe and wonder in miracles and elevated levels of apostolic anointing in manifestation. No greater example is needed of this than that of people being healed by the shadow of Peter (Acts 5:15). It is in this elevated manifestation of the anointing that immediate judgement is leveled upon Ananias and Sapphira resulting in death because they bold faced lied to God in the presence of profound anointing and manifestation.

This was not chastisement. This was not punishment. Instead, this was immediate *judgement*! This is not a passage to be understood as normative and applicable to the daily lives of believers. Yet, the message of the passage is palpable: Do not lie to God.

Begging the question then, what is chastisement, and how does it apply to an understanding of suffering salvation? After all, the writer of Hebrews emphatically declares that God, out of love, will chasten His children (Hebrew 12:6-8). In the same manner, the wisdom of Proverbs states, "because the Lord disciplines those he loves, as a father the son he delights in" (Proverbs 3:12). Likewise, John writes in the Revelation of Christ unto the church at Sardis declaring the Word of the Lord, "Those whom I love I rebuke and discipline. So be earnest and repent" (Revelation 3:19). Thus, an all-encompassing definition of chastisement does not equal punishment of sin. However, chastisement is a biblical aspect that should not be glossed over out of contemporary convenience.

So, the question remains: What is chastisement? A close examination of the Greek word for chastisement employed by the author of Hebrews discloses invaluable insight (Hebrews 12:6-8). The Greek word for chastisement is *Paideia,* meaning tutorage: education or training, disciplinary correction, instruction, and nurture (Strong's, 1890, G3809). The implication from the original word employed for chastisement has nothing to do with punishment for sin! Accordingly, it is a word that resembles education and tutorage through discipline for the purpose of cultivation and the increase of virtue (Strong's, 1890, G3809).

Furthermore, the context of the passage is granted through the imagery of a father. It is the imagery of a father who loves his children enough to correct them when they are wrong, with the intension of an empowered future. Meanwhile, a correlating and affirming image concerning the idea of chastisement in the vein of a loving correcting father is found in Proverbs, "because the Lord disciplines those he loves, as a father the son he delights in" (Proverbs 3:12).

Similarly, a contextual cross reference concerning God as a Father is necessary to land upon a proper interpretation of chastisement, as Jesus portrays the Father as loving and compassionate,

> "Which of you, if your son asks for bread, will give him a stone? Or if he asks for a fish, will give him a snake? If you, then, though you are evil, know how to give good gifts to your children, how much more will your Father in heaven give good gifts to those who ask him (Matthew 7:9-11)!

This passage presents God as a good father! Furthermore, the letter of 1 John presents God as a loving father who loves His children, "So we know and rely on the love God has for us. God is love." (1 John 4:16). The notion of a good and loving father must be prevalent when interpreting passages, Old and New Testament alike, concerning chastisement.

Based on context, a line of separation must be drawn between punishment and chastisement. The former, as an act of justice, revealing wrath, and the latter, as an act of mercy and love (Jacob, n.d., para. 5). For people who are in Christ Jesus, there is no condemnation (Romans 8:1), and they can suffer no punishment for sin, but only chastisement (Jacob, n.d., para. 5). Where there is guilt, there is punishment. However, where guilt has been removed, there can be no punishment (Jacobs, n.d., para. 5). *This is powerful truth!*

Thus, when chastisement is examined through the Greek definition, through the context of a loving Father, and though the context of justification in Christ Jesus, it can be established that the chastening of God is discipline permitted in love when deemed necessary by God. For an additional understanding of when God might permit chastisement, a re-examination of Revelation 3:19 is necessary, "Those whom I love I rebuke and discipline. So be earnest and repent" (Revelation 3:19).

Notate the emphasis upon earnest repentance applied within this verse. The implication in this text is that God, as a loving father, permits discipline for correction when the believer refuses to repent. In other words, when a believer continues in sin, displaying a willful fashion and refusing to repent over a space of time, the loving Father may choose to apply discipline with the purpose of correction by permitting difficult circumstances to transpire. It is possible that various situations of suffering salvation can result from God passively permitting a troubling situation to transpire inattentive of His intervention, as a form of correction, when a believer continues in rebellion, refusing to repent.

What does a natural father, who is loving and kind, do when his child needs correction? Does a good and healthy model of parenting involve a deficiency of discipline? Parents who choose to spoil their children with no discipline typically raise nonfunctional spoiled adults. In the same manner, the highlighted texts affirm that God, as Father, will permit pain in various circumstances when His children refuse to repent with the expressed loving purpose of long-term and futuristic correction. It boils down to the essential element of willingness to repent. A child of God who maintains a posture of intentional sin absent of repentance may place themselves in a position where chastisement manifests.

Considering this parental picture brings to memory talks with dad. Those moments in childhood sitting on the bed while dad lovingly, yet firmly, provides direction and correction for acts of continued rebellion. Good fathers never ignore needed correction. Likewise, a good father will rebuke willful rebellion. Therefore, those talks with dad are uncomfortably necessary.

In the same manner, God is not harsh or evil. Furthermore, God does not punish believers for their sins, as Jesus took the punishment for sins upon the cross. Yet, God may allow, in diverse situations, suffering salvation in the form of correction when repentance is disregarded.

Suggesting that God may permit suffering salvation to manifest in the face of a willful refusal of repentance is not equal to the suggestion that God Himself orders moments of suffering salvation to unfold upon His children. The Bible specifically teaches that God does not send wicked acts upon people, "Surely God will never do wickedly, nor will the Almighty pervert justice" (Job 34:12 NKJV).

God does not order calamity. Away with foolish preaching that teaches the hammering hand of God! In the same way, the Bible declares that God does not tempt His people with sin, "When tempted, no one should say, 'God is tempting me.' For God cannot be tempted by evil, nor does he tempt anyone; but each person is tempted when they are dragged away by their own evil desire and enticed" (James 1:13-14). Experiences of suffering salvation are never the result of the directive of God. The hand of God does not bring pain and suffering. *God is not an abusive Father.*

Likewise, God is not a dictatorial Father who manipulates and micromanages with moments of divine anguish. However, a child of God who ignores conviction and refuses to repent of sin may welcome the hand of God in the permission of suffering salvation manifesting in the absence of His divine intervention with the intention of change, repentance, and virtue.

Are all situations of suffering salvation the result of God passively permitting pain as a form of correction? No. Just as previous discussions in our journey concerning various possibilities for suffering salvation have been detailed within this book, chastisement is equal in the result. Poor theology is the view that all moments of suffering salvation in the lives of believers stem from unrepented sins. As we often label them, Job's friends are harmful and serve as a distraction from the truth, casting all blame for suffering salvation upon the direct result of sin (Job 4-23). Such shoddy and shabby theology of blaming all suffering salvation upon chastisement leads to hurt and anger toward God and clouded thinking regarding suffering. However, is it possible that some situations of suffering salvation manifest as the more significant result of God permitting pain to materialize removed from His intervention as a manner of Fatherly correction? Yes.

The pivotal point of my journey into suffering salvation divulged within this book unremittingly undertakes the biblical concept that varying circumstances can contribute to suffering salvation due to clashing possibilities. Repeatedly, my theological response to suffering salvation maintains that there is no one-size-fits-all answer in the Bible. Likewise, the subsequent question remains in direct response to our discussion concerning chastisement: Is every moment of suffering salvation experienced in life due to a refusal to repent within the life of the believer? No. Conversely, are various accounts of suffering salvation the direct result of chastisement? Yes.

The source of suffering salvation must be individually examined in each occurrence to garner theological conclusions. For instance, rebuking demons, as a form of spiritual warfare, will not bring resolution to moments of suffering salvation if chastisement is taking place. Appropriately, the most robust faith in the world will not prevent free will actions in every circumstance. Similarly, a believer demonstrating a lack of faith cannot condemn God as being aloof and evil due to encounters of suffering salvation.

Herein lies the point of the argument: Each instance of suffering salvation must be evaluated in and of itself to determine a theological conclusion. The one-size-fits-all manner of guidance in the moments suffering salvation must discontinue. A holistic theological response to suffering must include numerous factors and possible circumstances. For that reason, not every moment of suffering salvation can be attributed to chastisement. However, responsible believers must acknowledge that specific experiences of suffering salvation are permitted as periods of loving chastisement from the perfect Father.

In the following chapter, our journey into comprehending suffering salvation will transition into a transient discussion concerning the examination room. At this point in our journey, personal self-examination will become worthwhile.

Chapter 8
THE EXAMINATION ROOM

Now that our journey into understanding suffering salvation has considered the six biblical possibilities concerning why God allows believers to experience unfortunate circumstances, a close consideration of choices must be brought to the surface. Referring in brief to the contemplation offered within chapter 2 of the book concerning free will, human beings have choices in terms of behavior and action.

For instance, to pray or not to pray is a human choice. To read the Bible and live by its wisdom is a human choice. Accordingly, refusing to read the Bible and live by its wisdom is a human choice. To accept Christ as savior and follow Him is a human choice. To reject Christ as savior is a human choice. Strengthening faith and speaking the promises of the Word of God over yourself and your family is a behavioral choice.

In contrast, the decision to permit faith to be weak and weary, resulting in a lack of biblical promises being fulfilled practically, is equally a human choice. Engaging successfully in spiritual warfare is a human choice, and the refusal to fight spiritual battles, often resulting in disastrous defeat, is simultaneously a human choice. Trusting God or refusing to trust God is a human choice. Heeding the wisdom of friends and family is a human choice. Meanwhile, the decision to reject tried and true wisdom is a human choice.

Continuing in the vein of the articulation, driving a vehicle 40 miles beyond the speed limit resulting in loss of control and collision, is a human choice. Smoking cigarettes and developing lung cancer is a human choice. Drinking alcohol and developing liver disease is a human choice. Having sex outside of marriage resulting in emotional pain, separation from children, divorce, and financial hardship, is a human choice. It is not God's fault if poor human choices contribute to unfortunate suffering salvation.

Likewise, Satan cannot be blamed if the credit card debt is out of control resulting in a poor credit score and dilapidated housing. Choices in life often lead to the results that are experienced within life. *We must take responsibility for our decisions!*

Even so, God cannot be reproached for all accounts of suffering salvation when human behavioral choices are often the sincere culprit. The numerous examples concerning suffering salvation highlighted within this chapter are simplistic in explanation, even though they are difficult enough a pill to swallow. In several situations, suffering salvation can be summed by the consequences of human behavior. In other words, the question of why suffering salvation occurs can often be answered by free will and the choice of behavior.

The psychological teaching of maintaining a healthy self-monitor or self-awareness can explain self-attained suffering salvation and even recommend a remedy strategy for the future. Psychological self-monitor, by definition, is a personality trait reflecting an ability to modify one's behavior in response to situational pressures, opportunities, and norms (American Psychological Association, n.d., para. 2).

High self-monitors are typically more apt to conform their behavior to the demands of the situation, whereas low self-monitors tend to behave in accord with their internal feelings. In other words, people with a high self-monitor pay attention to their behavior on higher levels and adjust accordingly. Hence, paying attention to self-behavior and actions can promote future correction and positive direction. The decision to be self-aware and in control of choices and behavior can provide an enhanced life. The point is poignant within the discussion of suffering salvation due to the reality that often choices lead to agony, of which God is the object of the charge. *God is frequently falsely blamed for suffering!*

On the opposite side of the coin, however, there are situations in which suffering salvation is obviously out of the hands of personal choice. For example, a believer may affirm that they have developed solid faith built up and edified by the Word of God (Romans 10:17). Conversely, they may maintain a testimony of dealing with a horrific account of suffering salvation, nonetheless. Some Christians experience suffering even though they have strong faith!

Another Christian may testify that they waged an intense spiritual battle employing all of the tools that the Word teaches concerning victorious spiritual warfare (Ephesians 6:12-13).

Equally, they may insist that the heartache of suffering salvation persistently paraded itself into the situation. Pain is not always avoided, even though the devil is rebuked and the battle in won in the mind! A young Christian parent may proclaim that prayers were prayed, the Bible was quoted, and the enemy was rebuked, and still, their child passed away, notwithstanding.

When suffering salvation sneaks its way into the lives of believers in moments that extend beyond the responsibility of personal choice, a looming question remains: Why? Why does God allow suffering salvation to transpire within incredible moments? Why does a good God allow short caskets in Christian families? Why does a loving, all-powerful God permit heartache in the lives of believers? Why would God allow disabled children who love Jesus to be shot dead without cause? The answer to these pervasive questions resolves around this provocative argument made throughout this book: It depends.

My journey into understanding suffering salvation provides that each circumstance of suffering, outlined in detail within the previous chapters, hosts a variety of possibilities. There is no one-line answer casting a blanketed solution for all experiences of suffering salvation. Truthfully, each instance of suffering salvation needs honest self-examination through the lens of the six biblical possibilities suggested within this book. In other words, there must be a self-examination of each instance of suffering salvation to discover the truth of the reasons for the calamity. Thus, at this moment in our journey, we enter the examination room.

It must be noted that a strong sense of self-honesty is necessary to harvest a genuine self-examination for each circumstance of suffering salvation. Self-soothing, psychological coping, defensive barriers, denial, blame-shifting, and plain dishonesty will not discover the "why factor" concerning suffering salvation. In contrast, a forthright examination of your personal experience of suffering salvation through the biblical examples presented within the book may prove to be enlightening, as emotional as the process may be. Yet, this portion of our journey requires self-honesty and personal reflection.

The examination room is a moment of self-discovery and self-honesty, in which you review your circumstance of suffering salvation through the six biblical possibilities for causation. This is the practical application moment of the book. This is where you apply what has been shared in an encounter of personal and private self-examination.

Accordingly, this is the opportunity presented within this book for personal growth, truth discovery, spiritual liberation, and internal healing. If you are asking why God permitted your entanglement of suffering salvation, then process your experience through the six biblical possibilities. Hence, allow yourself to consider your experience of suffering salvation through the lens of the six following biblical possibilities in order to seek discovery of why suffering salvation was potentially permitted within your life:

1. <u>Free Will</u>: Did suffering salvation transpire in your life due to a personal self-choice? If the answer is a sheepish yet honest yes, there is no need to proceed forward in discovering a response to "why" suffering salvation was experienced. Learn from the mistake of choices and refuse to repeat equal errors in the future. There is wise value in learning from past decisions. Refuse to allow past patterns to predict future outcomes. As challenging as it may be, cease the continuation of destructive patterns and

paths. Meanwhile, redirect the anger and hurt from your period of suffering salvation away from God when it can be determined through self-examination that personal decisions and behaviors welcomed the unfortunate event. In other words, God cannot be blamed for your poor choices.

However, does an honest and forthright self-examination of your experience of suffering salvation disclose that your painful moment occurred due to another person's free will choice? As uncomfortable as it is to consider, God will not intervene and circumvent every single intention of action and behavior of the people you engage with. The result of God evading all negative actions and behaviors of others to shield you from all harm in every aspect of life would effectively eradicate free will. Thus, the issue of free will could be the specific answer to why God permitted you to experience suffering salvation. Simultaneously, refuse to lose heart and live in fear (2 Timothy 1:7)! Every believer possesses the power to claim the promises of God, plead the blood of Jesus, and live close to God's protection (Psalm 91). Does this mean God will intervene and circumvent all potential interpersonal harm from others in all situations? No. However, it does mean that believers can trust God and believe in protection knowing that free will is a reality that cannot be eradicated.

2. <u>The Big Picture</u>: Did suffering salvation occur in your life due to God's infinite knowledge compared to your limited knowledge? As challenging and emotional as it may be,

process your experience of suffering salvation through the lens of God, knowing more than you about the unknown details of the situation. God is good. God is love. However, God holds all knowledge of all past, present, and future situations, as well as all potential actions and reactions of His intervention or lack of intervention. It is beyond feasible to consider the possibility that God permitted your suffering salvation for reasons beyond your logical conclusions. The dim light of human comprehension is often the catalyst for frustration in painful situations. Even so, the lack of human ability to see the hidden details of eternal actions and interventions does not equate to an aloof God absent of concern or empathy. The argument that the existence of pain is proof of the non-existence of God fails in a logical conclusion. In contrast, the reality of a divine all-knowing God permits the possibility of divine understanding bypassing flawed human knowledge. In other words, the answer to why God allows suffering salvation is, at times, due to God's infinite understanding of the big picture. Therefore, considering God's knowledge could be the specific answer to why God permitted you to experience suffering salvation. In examining your account of suffering salvation, is it possible that God allowed the pain due to God possessing knowledge of more significant details behind the scenes that remain unknown to you?

3. <u>The Faith Factor</u>: Did suffering salvation visit your life due to a lack of developed faith? As outlined in chapter 4 of the book, a lack of strong faith is often rebuked by Jesus in the Gospels. Clear instructions are found in the Bible

that the believer must take the personal responsibility to build and develop faith. Furthermore, weak faith was the specific rationale for the lack of miraculous and divine intervention in Jesus' hometown (Mark 6:5). On the other hand, Jesus teaches in the Gospels through specific word choice and explanation that many miracles recorded were the result of strong faith. This is the most challenging moment concerning the self-examination room. Therefore, it is strongly recommended that you do yourself justice as you process your experience of suffering salvation through the genuine lens of self-examination. Consider the following questions: Did you speak words of faith over your situation, or did you lose heart and speak words of doubt (Romans 4:17; Matthew 21:22)? Did you stand upon the promises of God, or did you believe the report of the world? Did you quote the promises of the Word in your life? Did you maintain a faith confession during the storm? All of the questions submitted deserve appropriate reflection in the examination room. A void of solid faith could be the answer to why God permitted suffering salvation to manifest in your specific circumstances. Faith is the bridge to access the movement and intervention of God (Hebrews 11:6; Matthew 21:21). Conversely, if your self-examination through the lens of faith determines that your faith was strong concerning your experience of suffering salvation and that you did stand firm upon the promises of God, then weak faith can be crossed out as a culprit in your encounter of suffering salvation. Contrary to popular belief within the extreme ends of faith teaching, faith is *not* always the diagnosis

SUFFERING SALVATION

for suffering salvation. Poor theology casts blame for all suffering upon weak faith! Thus, only your honest self-examination concerning faith can yield accurate results reflecting suffering salvation.

4. The Trials of Life: Did suffering salvation manifest in your life as the result of fiery trials? Examine your experience of suffering salvation through the comprehensive lens of growth through pressure. *Pain and pressure often produce the process necessary for growth and maturity.* In the same vein, examine your encounter of suffering salvation through the metaphor of refining gold, seeking the extraction of poor elements. Does an honest self-evaluation of your entanglement with suffering salvation disclose a lesson to be learned in the fire? God permits suffering salvation in various situations to bring strength, transformation, introspection, and resolve to the believer. Suffering is presented within scripture as having an empowering and refining effect. Fiery trials have a transformational repercussion on the believer. The Bible says that the trying of the faith produces patience (James 1:2-3). Accordingly, some lessons in life cannot be learned outside of the fiery trial. Likewise, some aspects of introspection and self-enhancement are the benefits of suffering, which are seldom discovered in other forms. The trials of life hold the end goal of enhancing the believer. Period. Suffering serves, in various situations, to build the believer's resolve. Most often, a lesson is learned while the battle rages. As you apply self-examination concerning your experience of suffering salvation through the lens of refinement,

can you discover a strength that was absent before the encounter? In contrast, it must be underscored that all periods of suffering salvation do not stem from the fiery trial and lessons of refinement. Narrow-minded theology summarizes every account of suffering salvation to the attribution of the fiery trial. Thus, poor preaching concludes every moment of suffering found at the root of God, desiring the recipient to be molded and strengthened in the flames of fire. However, indeed, the answer to why God allows suffering salvation in various moments can be surmised by a transformation and resolve that can only be formed in the flame's heat. Meanwhile, the Bible is chalked full of examples that God's people will, at various times, endure temptation and hardship. Therefore, a transparent self-examination concerning the fiery trial may reveal why God permitted your account of suffering salvation.

5. Spiritual Warfare: Did suffering salvation arise in your life due to failed spiritual warfare? Understand the reality that Satan and demons are real. Likewise, if the enemy would have his way in your life, there would remain nothing except destruction and death (John 10:10; 1 Peter 5:8). Accordingly, the enemy is continuously seeking ways to devour your life and lead you into spiritual peril. Spiritual warfare must be waged in a real ongoing battle, and victory must be obtained by applying biblical principles in order for believers to experience practical success. Laziness in the spirit leads to defeat. Sloppy warfare contributes to disastrous action. As you apply self-examination to your encounter with suffering salvation through the lens of

spiritual warfare, is there clear evidence pointing to a lack of warfare principles contributing to the cause? Remember, the examination room requires honest self-exploration. As such, spiritual warfare is only victorious with adherence to strict maintenance of mental process and spoken words of authority in Jesus Christ. In practical terms, only positive, constructive thoughts can abide within the mind (Philippians 4:8). Lies must be guarded against and cast down (2 Corinthians 10:5-6). The enemy must be resisted in word and action (James 4:7). There must be an intentional and verbal declaration of the truth of the Word of God. In another terms, give the enemy zero wiggle room to work in your life. Is every instance of suffering salvation the result of Satan, demons, or the loss of warfare within the mind and mouth? No. However, a thorough self-examination must include asking yourself the taxing questions concerning whether a lack of successful spiritual warfare contributed to why God permitted the circumstance. Consequently, a translucent self-examination concerning spiritual warfare may generate an understanding of why God permitted your account of suffering salvation.

6. <u>A Talk with Dad</u>: Did suffering salvation break out in your life due to chastisement? God is a good father. God is not harsh or evil. Away with the poor theology that God punishes his people for their sins. However, chastisement is, in fact, a theological aspect with a solid foundation in the Bible that cannot be quietly dismissed from the examination room. While chastisement is not to be defined as a harsh punishment of sin, as outlined in chapter 7 of this

book, chastisement is a process of God allowing certain situations into the lives of believers to correct His children when deemed necessary. Forthrightly, when believers ignore God, His Word, and His conviction choosing to live a life complete with neglecting the principles of God, the good Father must seek to allow loving correction. Chastisement is not a process of God slaying people with pain. Conversely, it is a caring process in which God permits pain for fatherly correction. A genuine self-examination of suffering salvation would lack credibility without a determination concerning chastisement. Does every experience of suffering salvation stem from God's loving correction? No. Nonetheless, the Bible does point to examples where this, in fact, could be the root of the explanation. Thus, does the examination room reveal any circumstance concerning your experience of suffering salvation in which it is self-obvious that ignoring God, dismissing God's principles, or maintaining a refusal to repent of sin stand apparent? If so, chastisement could be the reason why there was permission for suffering salvation. How can believers deal with sin if an honest self-examination discloses unrepented sin or rebellion? Repent and ask for forgiveness through the shed blood of Jesus. Repentance is the answer to the need for forgiveness! God is merciful and forgiving to those who humble themselves and ask. The writer of 1 John says it best, "If we confess our sins, He is faithful and just and will forgive us our sins and purify us from all unrighteousness" (1 John 1:9). Call upon the name of Jesus and receive healing and forgiveness from the one and only merciful God!

Suffering Salvation

7. <u>The Trust Zone</u>: Finally, what happens if the examination room reveals no conclusion that honestly applies to your circumstances in suffering salvation? In other words, what if a self-examination through the six biblical lenses for suffering yields no return on your encounter? Where do you go for a theological response if your moment of suffering remains unexplainable beyond the terms provided within the six lenses of discussion? The answer is to take a step of faith and trust. In times such as these, you take a step of faith and simply trust in God's goodness and infinite knowledge. God is good. God is just. God is perfect. God is love. God is kind. God is merciful. Moreover, God only has good intentions for your life (Jeremiah 29:11). However, there are moments within the believer's life when unexplainable situations will transpire, causing trust in the goodness of God to be showcased. Faith is trust in God. Period. Every thorny rose will not be delivered entirely with a full download of divine explanation. Accordingly, trust must be the mantra of the believer during inexplicable periods of suffering salvation, knowing that God only extends the best of determinations for His children. The aspect of trust was not a standalone chapter within the book and was not a specific portion of the self-examination. Nevertheless, when zero understanding of suffering salvation can be observed, a simplistic trust in God is all that is required. Healing for the wounded heart is extended when trust in God is displayed. The wisdom of Proverbs says it best, "Trust in the Lord with all your heart, and do not lean on your own understanding" (Proverbs 3:5 ESV).

Did you apply honest self-examination of your pain encounter through the lens provided? If so, what are your self-concluding extractions from the examination room concerning your experience of pain?

Overall, the answer to why God allows suffering salvation is as follows: It depends. There are a host of varying determinizing factors that could offer an explanation as to why God allows suffering salvation. Why God permits suffering must be answered by examining the circumstances in analysis with the biblical patterns outlined. Why God allows suffering salvation does not have to be a mysterious question filled with heavenly wonder. Furthermore, why God permits suffering salvation in the lives of people who love Him does not need to be concluded with the belief that God is evil, mean, aloof, manipulative, spiteful, or punishing.

In the same manner, the existence of suffering salvation is by no means proof of the non-existence of God. To suggest that God is not real due to God allowing evil or pain is an illogical leap to a conclusion based upon personal convenience. Instead, it stands to reason that God has multiple possible circumstances in which God, in His infinite understanding, permits periods of pain. Meanwhile, the answer to why God allows suffering salvation can be examined through the lens of the six biblical possibilities to provide insight into the potential understanding of your suffering.

In the following chapter, our journey into comprehending suffering salvation will conclude with a final stop considering new thoughts and realigned comprehension concerning suffering salvation.

Chapter 9
FINAL THOUGHTS

Upon the conclusion of any excellent sermon, the listener should have some take-home material. A quality sermon must offer something that applies to the listener's life in a practical or meaningful fashion. Truly, a sermon that goes in a hundred random directions absent of practical clarity is a failure on the part of the preacher. Many potential sermons implode due to rabbit trail fogginess.

Accordingly, preachers who brag about adding a hundred directions to a message inadvertently embarrass themselves. Good preaching follows a flow of the Spirit. However, good preaching also brings clarity to the message. In other words, there must be a "So What" applicability to a sermon for the message to bring authentic change to the lives of the listener.

In a sermon or book, what is unnecessary is additional material stacked upon the convoluted collection of unusable information swirling within everyday life. People are consumed daily with insignificant and meaningless messages. Therefore, allow our journey into understanding suffering salvation to arrive upon a destination of practical application, genuine benefit, and insightful extraction.

The primary purpose of this book is to cast additional biblical light into the existing literature concerning the conversation of why God allows believers to suffer and to provide aching hearts with a measurement of hope, help, and healing concerning the theological response to moments of suffering salvation. Through the process of sharing insight gained through personal study and reflection initially propelled by my testimony of the loss of our firstborn baby, this book is my addition to the colossal collection of literature concerning Christians and suffering.

Thus, I believe that the six examples from scripture presented concerning various patterns of possibilities of suffering salvation eliminate singularity of response. There must be a cease-fire in the practical theology of attempting to explain suffering salvation to hurting believers with one category of response. Believers need an expanded view of the reasons for suffering in place of a singular mantra.

Hence, the answer extended in this argument for why God allows suffering salvation in the lives of people who love Him is as follows: It depends. Prayerfully, the examination room found in chapter 8 will provide personal reflection in addition to this book's theological argumentation, which seeks to provide a theological response to suffering.

However, as our journey ends, I must go one step further in this book. To those who find themselves lost in sin and broken by the sinful decisions of free will, God is willing to forgive if you will submit unto Him. Likewise, forgiveness for the rebellious is available for anyone who asks God in faith believing (1 John 1:9;

John 3:16; Romans 10:9-10; Romans 10:13; Isaiah 55:7; Matthew 18:21-22; Acts 3:19).

In addition, for the believer who maintains sin and is concerned about suffering moments for a wide array of reasons, call upon God and ask for forgiveness. God is a forgiver and a lover of humanity. Thus, look to God in sincere sorrow of sin, and He will forgive.

On the other hand, the hurting heart that has been battered, bruised, and busted due to the agony of loss in suffering salvation must recognize the hope and healing that is available in Jesus Christ. Upon this notion, Jesus cries out to any hurting heart who will respond to Him in faith,

> "Come to me, all you who are weary and burdened, and I will give you rest. Take my yoke upon you and learn from me, for I am gentle and humble in heart, and you will find rest for your souls. For my yoke is easy and my burden is light" (Matthew 11:28-30).

Jesus is the healer of the hurting heart, not the one who hurts the heart. *Read that again!* In the prophetic revelation of the savior, the prophet Isaiah declares Him to be the healer of the internal wounds (Isaiah 53:5). Emotional brokenness does not have to be the position following suffering. Furthermore, the Bible shares hope concerning the inner healing power of God, "He heals the brokenhearted and binds up their wounds" (Psalm 147:3). Therefore, if suffering salvation has left you internally bound and bruised, then call upon the name of the healer, Jesus Christ, and receive His internal mending. Healing is available to those who can humble themselves and request internal help in faith believing.

On the other hand, if suffering salvation has leveled you with displaced anger aimed upward toward the highest essence of authority, release your blame from His Holy name. Understandably, negative emotions of anger and heartache directed toward God for His allowance of your pain are common and human dispositions. Indeed, God contains all power and ability to intervene and prevent all acts of suffering salvation. This divine factor often generates anger and confusion to be lifted in God's direction from believers in agony.

About my first encounter of suffering salvation presented within chapter 1 of this book, I invested more than a year of my life following our baby's death, wrestling with anger and an overwhelming sense of hurt directed toward God for His perceived passive allowance of our suffering. However, the pain of suffering salvation did not end with our first occurrence. While still reeling from burying our first baby, our second pregnancy ended in an early-term miscarriage.

Then, I suffered the sharp pain of broken bones when my wife and I were involved in a violent vehicle collision. If that was not enough, my wife was then diagnosed with breast cancer following the birth of our third and only living child. Even though she defeated cancer, suffering was not absent from the process. The list of suffering salvation continues as several trials have been persistent in life. Accordingly, these events transpired in our lives while we maintained faith, prayed in a healthy fashion, did scripture confession, and served as a full-time pastors.

In other words, I can personally identify with the misdirected frustration pointed at the almighty God in response to the anguish of suffering salvation. It is normal to temporarily wrestle with hurt emotions; however, living with them is unhealthy. Refuse to normalize pain. Instead, release the pain to the one who can heal the pain.

In my journey into understanding a theological response to why God permits believers to suffer discovered a wide array of possibilities providing freedom from the mental trap produced by the enemy. God is not unfaithful to His Word. Satan and demons would love to confuse believers into believing God is aloof and cruel. However, God is nothing except for love, grace, and mercy.

God is faithful, and every instance of permitted pain comes with a potential divine reason, as outlined within the various biblical examples of explanation. When reconciliation cannot be discovered, trust in the divine nature of the loving God of glory.

Overall, I learned to release the hurt in prayer. Thus, enter your prayer closet and tell God in honest words exactly how you feel while describing the pain and the perceived viewpoint of divine passivity. God is big enough to handle frank, reverent, and respectful prayers in which you release your hurt and anger. God can take it. Following prayer and submission unto God, rest within the goodness of God, knowing that He offers freedom and healing from the pain.

Additionally, allow the diverse understandings presented within this book to provide comprehension into the "why" for suffering salvation. A theological response can give the reflection, consideration, and critical application that is often necessary for some believers to advance healthily beyond the agony of the moment of suffering. Therefore, this book's intention is for theological reflection to provide a sense of realistic reinforcement.

In closing, the following rapid-fire review points are my final thoughts presented in the practical application intended for a broadened comprehension concerning suffering salvation:

1. Suffering salvation does not always occur because of Satan and demons. It is poor theology to believe that *all* suffering salvation manifests as the result of demons. Yes, some experiences of suffering salvation are demonic. However, not every instance of suffering salvation finds its root in demonic activity. Rebuking the devil is a waste of energy that will not cease moments of suffering salvation *if another root* is the cause. Cease blaming the devil for every battle!

2. Suffering salvation does not always occur because of a lack of faith. It is shameful to beat people down who have experienced suffering salvation with the misguided biblical bat of faith. Yes, some instances of suffering salvation are the result of weak faith. However, faith does not suffice as a singular cause of suffering. Cease claiming weak faith as the solitary trigger for suffering salvation!

3. Suffering salvation does not always occur because of the refiner's fire. It is shoddy theology to counsel *every* hurting believer with the unseasoned words that God is allowing the pain to bring forth pure gold. God is a refiner, and *some* instances of suffering salvation result from fiery trials intended to strengthen and reform. Suffering is presented within scripture as having an empowering and refining effect. Fiery trials have a transformational repercussion on the believer. However, cease believing that each instance of suffering salvation is a fiery trial!

4. Suffering salvation does not always occur because of sin. The indication that a believer is suffering at the hand of an angry God is a lie that originates from Hell. Jobs friends are cruel church bullies that need to be silenced. Yes, sin can lead to suffering salvation in *some* circumstances. However, it is spiritually and psychologically harmful to state that all suffering salvation is sin-ridden. Cease listening to church bullies who blame all suffering salvation upon sin!
5. Suffering salvation is not proof that God is aloof. The conclusion that suffering salvation is evidence that God is distant, disconnected, or detached is an unfounded leap to a conclusion. In opposition, the existence of suffering proves nothing concerning God. Humans are limited and shortsighted, whereas God is unlimited and infinite. If the limited human who does not know all things concludes that the unlimited God who does know all things is aloof due to a period of suffering, an illogical determination has been established. God never promised His people would be free from all pain and harm on this Earth. Conversely, the belief that suffering proves God to be aloof is quite egocentric and selfish. Cease the bourgeois belief that God guarantees gold streets and lives of ease upon Earth!
6. Is all suffering salvation the fault of the believer? It depends. In some circumstances, suffering salvation can be human-induced. Yet, in other cases, suffering is *not* at all human-induced. What if an honest self-examination of your experience with suffering salvation concludes that self-failure was a contributing factor? A biblical response

would be to take responsibility and avoid the next self-inflicting wound! For instance, if weak faith was the cause of suffering salvation, then be responsible and build up your faith. If sin contributed to suffering salvation, repent of sin and go in a different direction. If suffering salvation results from failure to wage spiritual warfare, then learn from the Word and begin waring in the spirit. If suffering salvation is the result of the refiner's fire, then learn what was intended from the fire. If suffering salvation, in your situation, was the result of poor choices, then take responsibility and make better choices. Stop making excuses for self-induced suffering salvation, and begin taking responsibility!

7. What is a healthy response when suffering salvation is not the believer's fault? Trust God. Release your hurting heart into the hands of the healer. In moments of pain, cling to His presence. In situations of suffering, surrender to His sovereignty. On days of disappointment, trust His divinity. In other words, present your pain to God in prayer. God is love. God is goodness. God is grace. God is mercy. Refuse to run away from the only one who holds the day! The apostle Paul presents the utmost realization concerning trusting God in the midst of suffering salvation as he states, "I consider that our present sufferings are not worth comparing with the glory that will be revealed in us" (Romans 8:18).

This journey concludes with the exhortation of the psalmist as troublesome days presented themselves as a present reality,

"I lift up my eyes to the mountains—where does my help come from? My help comes from the Lord, the Maker of heaven and earth. He will not let your foot slip - he who watches over you will not slumber; indeed, he who watches over Israel will neither slumber nor sleep. The Lord watches over you—the Lord is your shade at your right hand; the sun will not harm you by day, nor the moon by night. The Lord will keep you from all harm—he will watch over your life; the Lord will watch over your coming and going both now and forevermore" (Psalm 121).

REFERENCES

American Psychological Association. (n.d.). APA Dictionary of Psychology. https://dictionary.apa.org/self-monitoring

Armstrong, D. (2019). Did God immorally murder King David's innocent child? Pathes.com. https://www.patheos.com/blogs/davearmstrong/2019/05/did-god-immorally-murder-king-davids-innocent-child.html

Arvanitis, J. (2003). *Pankration: The traditional Greek combat sport and modern mixed martial art*. Paladin Press.

Bible Study Tools. (n.d). Ephesians 6:12. Commentary. https://www.biblestudytools.com/commentaries/gills-exposition-of-the-bible/ephesians-6-12.html

Britannica, T. Editors of Encyclopedia (2014). *Conflict*. Encyclopedia Britannica. https://www.britannica.com/science/conflict-psychology

Brown, N. (2013). New atheism and the problem of evil. Black River Technical College. ProQuest.

https://www.proquest.com/docview/1366045294?parent
SessionId=FJsmG3DxTEhinhj%2FszARJZEZzqUb7Fq9JU
XKpSLb%2FNQ%3D

Calvin, J. *Institutes*. Book 1 Chapter 16. Christian History Institute. https://christianhistoryinstitute.org/study/module/calvin-on-gods-sovereignty

Chick, N. (n.d.). Metacognition. Vanderbilt University Center for Teaching.
https://cft.vanderbilt.edu/guides-sub-pages/metacognition/

Cherry, K. (2021). 20 Common defense mechanisms used for anxiety. Very Well Mind.
https://www.verywellmind.com/defense-mechanisms-2795960

Chrysostom, J. (n.d.). Chrysostom: Early church's greatest preacher. Christianity Today.
https://www.christianitytoday.com/history/people/pastorsandpreachers/john-chrysostom.html

Cox, T. (2020). Transforming cyclical conflict which impedes church revitalization. [Thesis]. Lee University.

English Standard Version. (2008). Bible Gateway. www.biblegateway.com (Original Published Date 2008).

Greathouse, W. (2008). *Romans 1-8: A commentary in the Wesleyan tradition*. Beacon Hill Press of Kansas City.

Hall, C. (2002). *Learning theology with the church fathers*. IVP Academic.

Jacobs, H. (n.d.). Chastening: chastisement. Bible Study Tools.com https://www.biblestudytools.com/dictionary/chastening-chastisement/

Johnson, L. (2010). *The writings of the New Testament*. 3rd Edition. Fortress Press.

Ledden, P. (2018). 15 types of distorted thinking, 12/15: Blaming. Abate Counseling and EAP Limited. https://abatecounselling.ie/2018/11/23/blaming/

McKim, D. (1996). *Westminster dictionary of theological terms*. Westminster John Knox Press.

New International Version. (2001). Bible Gateway. www.biblegateway.com (Original Published Date 1973).

New Kings James Version. (1982). Bible Gateway. www.biblegateway.com (Original Published Date 1982).

Palmer, P. (2020). What is the refiner's fire in Malachi? Biblestudytools.com. https://www.biblestudytools.com/bible-study/topical-studies/what-is-the-refiners-fire-in-malachi.html

Rees, T. (n.d.). Believers. Bible Study Tools.com. https://www.biblestudytools.com/dictionary/believers/

Stanford Encyclopedia of Philosophy. (2015). The problem of evil. https://plato.stanford.edu/entries/evil/

Strong, J. (1890). *Strong's online concordance.* https://www.eliyah.com/lexicon.html

Spurgeon, C. (1855). C. H. Spurgeon: Chastisement. Blue Letter Bible. https://www.blueletterbible.org/Comm/spurgeon_charles/sermons/0048.cfm

Thayer and Smith. (1999). *Pistis*. The Bible Study Tools New Testament Greek Lexicon. https://www.biblestudytools.com/lexicons/greek/nas/pistis.html

Therapy Now SF. (2021). The fallacy of fairness: An overview of this cognitive distortion. https://www.therapynowsf.com/blog/the-fallacy-of-fairness-an-overview-of-this-cognitive-distortion

Thomas, D. (n.d.). A pastoral theology of suffering. Reformed Faith and Practice. https://journal.rts.edu/article/a-pastoral-theology-of-suffering/

Young, A. (2017). The holy fathers on illness. Orthodox Christianity. https://orthochristian.com/106274.html

Yount, W. (2010). *Created to learn: A Christian teacher's introduction to educational psychology.* 2nd Edition. B&H Books. https://app.logos.com/books/LLS%3A9781433672811/references/page.547

Made in United States
North Haven, CT
13 May 2023

36527921R00088